DELIGHTFUL INNS OFF THE

DELIGHTFUL INNS OFF THE BEATEN TRACK

The West Country

Peter Andrew Lyne

Pen and ink drawings by Juliet Greaves

EX LIBRIS PRESS

First published in 1989 by
Ex Libris Press
1 The Shambles
Bradford on Avon
Wiltshire

Cover by 46 Design, Bradford on Avon
Typeset in Plantin by Saxon Printing Ltd., Derby
Printed in Great Britain by BPCC Wheatons Ltd, Exeter

ISBN 0 948578 13 0

CONTENTS

AUTHOR'S INTRODUCTION

I hope you will have a lot of interest, and fun, tracking down this selection of delightful inns, many of them in remote corners of the West Country. I have deliberately excluded establishments in towns and cities, and those lying on or near *A* roads. A few are on *B* roads, but most are reached via the country lanes for which rural England is famous.

Although the title refers to "Delightful Inns", the book actually contains a mixture of inns and pubs (a pub often being thought of as an "inn without accommodation"), plus a few small hotels which offer meals and snacks to non-residents. About half the places described here offer at least limited accommodation, and the rest are simply pubs.

There is something rather special about finding an inn or pub in a delightful rural setting, uncluttered by city or main road traffic, or by too many chance visitors. My own interest is not so much the details of food, drink, or accommodation, as the total setting – the feel of the place and its surroundings. Most "Big Name" guides, with their tendency to standardised descriptions and a lack of illustrations, seem to me to fail in this important respect. So I have tried to give a miniature, but sensitive, portrait of each inn and its country setting. Please bear in mind that I have visited most places at lunchtime, often in the middle of the week. This means that the book's emphasis is on pub-like facilities, rather than accommodation or formal restaurant meals.

Many of the inns are thoroughly off the beaten track. They require some map-reading skills, and a pleasure in tackling narrow country lanes. I hope this special feature of the book will appeal to walkers and cyclists as well as motorists. However, if you are motoring please be warned that the lanes, although invariably well-surfaced, require patience and care. Realistic average speeds for the last part of your journey may be no more than ten miles per hour.

I have visited all the inns personally during 1988, and the descriptions are my own. The only exception is the information about Opening Hours, Meals, Drinks, and so on, given immediately under the photograph or drawing of each inn. In many cases this has been obtained from a questionnaire returned to me by the inn itself.

All inns were visited anonymously. Having decided that I wished to include a particular one, I wrote to the manager to ask permission. No inclusion fee was charged, but I requested a contribution towards author's travel expenses, to be paid at the time of publication. It was made clear right from the start that any such payment was entirely voluntary and in no way influenced inclusion. To further safeguard editorial independence, no advertising has been accepted, nor have the inns themselves had any say in the book's contents.

Such independence offers a major advantage. The rather cloying descriptions found in many inn and pub guides can be avoided, and an attempt made to be frank and fair. If parking is very limited, or the toilets are below standard, I think my readers ought to know. A unique feature of this book – as far as I am aware – is the Star-Rating system used to summarise such facilities. I hope you will find them honest and consistent. I have also commented briefly on wheelchair access, for any of my readers who are disabled. I am not an expert on this, but hope my remarks will prove helpful. I would just add that all the inns described here are, in my view, delightful. Any criticisms should be seen in this overall context.

Of course delightfulness is a many-sided virtue. Some inns possess it on account of their buildings, atmosphere, or excellent facilities; others on account of their rural setting or surroundings. The one thing you may be sure of is that all have something special to offer, and all are more or less off the beaten track.

Inns and pubs are living institutions, subject to development and change. Landlords move, cooks retire. The legal and social framework within which they operate is far from static. It is therefore possible that some of the information in this book will be out-of-date by the time you read it. I can only say that I have tried to be accurate, and would be pleased to receive any readers' comments on the form included at the end of the book.

It just remains for me to wish you as much enjoyment in finding the inns as I have had, and some safe and pleasant journeys.

P.A.L.

FINDING YOUR WAY

The next two pages contain Master Maps, accurate to within a few miles, showing the whereabouts of all inns described in this book. Then, turning to a particular inn description, you will find a detailed map covering a 4x4 mile area in the immediate vicinity. This is drawn to a scale of about 1:125,000 (1/2 inch to the mile), and shows all surfaced roads including narrow country lanes. The inn is indicated by a large letter "I", joined to a black blob which gives the precise location. A brief route description is also given (it generally covers one possible route, whereas most inns can of course be approached from several directions!).

Before consulting the detailed map you may find it helpful to refer to one of the standard motorists' maps of Great Britain, such as the AA, RAC, or Geographers' atlases which have a scale of about a quarter inch to the mile. They are widely available in bookshops and newsagents.

For those of you wishing to use the highly accurate Ordnance Survey (O.S.) 1:50,000 maps, the relevant sheet number and 6-figure map reference of the inn are also given.

MASTER MAPS

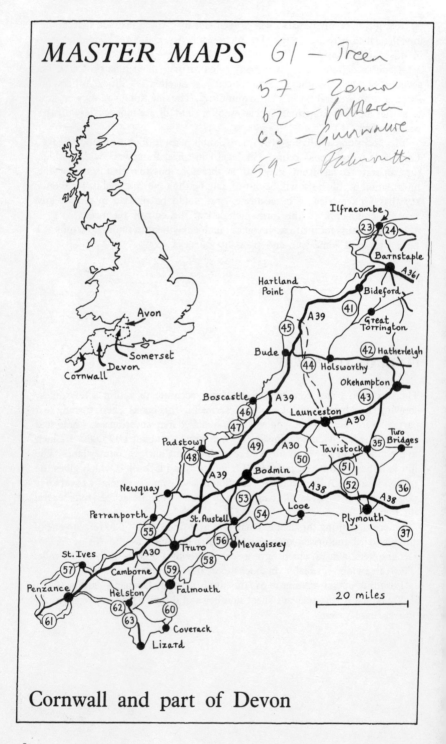

61 — Treen
57 — Zennor
62 — Portheras
65 — Gunwalloe
59 — Falmouth

Ilfracombe
23 24
Barnstaple
A361
Hartland
Point
Bideford
A39 41
Great
Torrington
45
Bude 42 Hatherleigh
44 Holsworthy
Okehampton
Boscastle A39 43
46
Launceston A30
47
Padstow 49 A30 Tavistock 35 Two Bridges
48 50
Bodmin 51
Newquay A39 52 36
53 A38 A38
Perranporth 54 Looe Plymouth
55 St. Austell 37
St. Ives 56 Mevagissey
A30 Truro
57 Camborne 58
Penzance 59
Helston Falmouth 20 miles
62
61 63 60
Coverack
Lizard

Cornwall and part of Devon

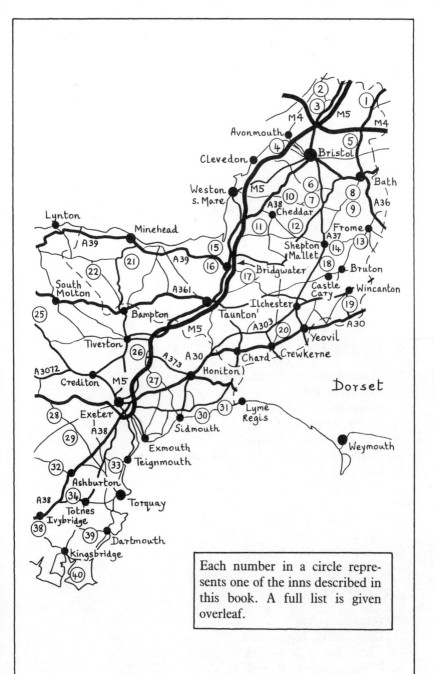

Each number in a circle represents one of the inns described in this book. A full list is given overleaf.

Avon, Somerset, and part of Devon

MASTER LIST

Below are listed all the inns, pubs, and small hotels featured in this book. Each is given a number, which is used both on the Master Maps, and in the main body of the book.

AVON

1. Fleece Inn, Hillesley
2. Anchor Inn, Oldbury on Severn
3. Fox Inn, Old Down
4. Black Horse, Clapton in Gordano
5. Bull, Hinton
6. Druids Arms, Stanton Drew
7. Pony and Trap, Newtown, Chew Magna
8. Wheatsheaf, Combe Hay
9. Fox and Badger, Wellow
10. New Inn, Blagdon

SOMERSET

11. Wheatsheaf Inn, Stone Allerton
12. New Inn, Priddy
13. White Hart, Trudoxhill
14. Strode Arms, Cranmore
15. Old Ship Inn, Combwich
16. Lamb Inn, Four Forks, Spaxton
17. George Inn, Middlezoy
18. Manor House Inn, Ditcheat
19. Half Moon Inn, Horsington
20. Cat Head, Chiselborough
21. Royal Oak Inn, Luxborough
22. Royal Oak Inn, Withypool

DEVON

23. Grampus, Lee
24. Olde Globe, Berrynarbor
25. Exeter Inn, Chittlehamholt
26. Butterleigh Inn, Butterleigh
27. Five Bells, Clyst Hydon
28. Bullers Arms, Chagford
29. Ring of Bells, North Bovey

30. Masons Arms, Branscombe
31. Ship Inn, Axmouth
32. Tavistock Inn, Poundsgate
33. Wild Goose, Combeinteignhead
34. Church House Inn, Rattery
35. Peter Tavy Inn, Peter Tavy
36. Mountain Inn, Lutton
37. Mildmay Colours Inn, Holbeton
38. First and Last, Ermington
39. Normandy Arms, Blackawton
40. Millbrook Inn, South Pool
41. Coach and Horses Inn, Buckland Brewer
42. Half Moon Inn, Sheepwash
43. Clovelly Inn, Bratton Clovelly
44. Bridge Inn, Bridgerule

CORNWALL

45. Bush Inn, Morwenstow
46. Mill House Inn, Trebarwith
47. Portgaverne Hotel, Portgaverne
48. Cornish Arms, St. Merryn
49. Old Inn, St. Breward
50. Crows Nest Inn, Crows Nest
51. Carpenters Arms, Metherell
52. Spaniards Inn, Cargreen
53. Crown, Lanlivery
54. Fishermans Arms, Golant
55. Miners Arms, Mithian
56. Crown Inn, St. Ewe
57. Tinners Arms, Zennor
58. Lugger Hotel, Portloe
59. Pandora Inn, Restronguet Passage
60. Five Pilchards Inn, Porthallow
61. Logan Rock Inn, Treen
62. Ship Inn, Porthleven
63. Halzephron Inn, Gunwalloe

NOTES

Below each inn photograph or drawing you will find information on Opening Hours, Meals, Beer and Wine, Childrens' Facilities, and so on, supplied in most cases by the inn itself. The following notes explain something of the background to this information.

OPENING HOURS

The law on opening hours was relaxed in 1988, allowing inns and pubs to stay open all day, except on Sundays. Needless to say this is seen as a mixed blessing by many landlords and managers, because of the problem of staffing. About a third of all inns and pubs have so far decided to extend opening hours at least to some extent – often by remaining open throughout Saturday afternoons. This is much more likely to apply in tourist and holiday areas, and in the summer months.

The current situation is fluid. If you are travelling far and intend to arrive at a nonstandard hour, it would be sensible to check in advance to avoid disappointment.

FOOD

I decided early on that I would not attempt to make this book a "Food Guide". Proper assessment of an inn's food would involve sampling various meals and snacks, at weekends and in midweek, in and out of the holiday season. Unfortunately this was not practicable, so although I have occasionally commented on meals and menus, I have not done so on a systematic basis. Instead I have simply indicated the days and times at which meals and snacks are served.

Almost all the inns featured here offer good snacks (hot and cold) and meals at reasonable prices. Many of them have restaurants, as well as serving bar food. If you are intending to have a substantial meal it is certainly a good idea to telephone in advance to ask about menus, and to book a table. Remember that the better an inn's food, the more likely it is to be busy – especially during holiday periods and at weekends.

DRINK

I realise that many visitors to inns and pubs are connoisseurs of beer, and an increasing number are connoisseurs of wine. I am no great expert myself, and anyway since I generally travelled by car I could not test alcoholic drinks properly. Instead I have simply asked each inn to give the names of a few beers they stock, and are proud of. If a particular establishment is currently recommended by the Campaign for Real Ale (CAMRA), I have indicated the fact by an asterisk (*) against the list of beers. As far as wines are concerned, I have asked each pub whether it serves wines by the glass, has a proper wine list, and offers house wines in carafe. If a wine list is indicated, I think you may assume that the matter of wine is taken reasonably seriously!

12

CHILDRENS' FACILITIES

The current situation regarding children in inns and pubs is confusing. Legally, children under 14 are not allowed in bars or areas where alcohol is served. However enforcement of this rule is very variable, both from county to county and even from one pub to the next. In some cases a room is specially put aside for children and families – although it must be said that it may not be particularly attractive. Also, many pubs have gardens or other outside areas, and these are generally (though by no means universally) suitable for children.

If I have not noted the availability of a Family Room or garden suitable for children, it does not necessarily mean that children are unwelcome. In many cases no objection is raised to them being in an eating area, providing they are accompanied by adults and are reasonably quiet and well-behaved. If you are in doubt about this, I suggest telephoning in advance to clarify the situation, remembering that the management of the inn must be allowed to exercise its own discretion.

Finally, it is worth bearing in mind that for every person who would like to take children into a pub or inn, there is someone else who would prefer it to remain a place for adults only. In practice it seems that the attitude towards children is largely determined by the management, and comes to be accepted by the local population over a considerable period.

DOGS

Attitudes towards dogs vary widely. At one extreme, dogs may not be welcome either in the bars, or in the garden. At the other (probably when the landlord or manager is a dog-owner), they may be given free rein. Perhaps the most typical situation is when dogs are allowed in the garden or outside area, and inside (if on a lead) at the landlord's discretion. Unless the information clearly states that dogs are welcome, you would be wise to assume that at least some restrictions apply.

ACCOMMODATION

About half the establishments listed in this book offer accommodation – ranging from just one or two rooms to perhaps twelve or fifteen. A few are primarily small hotels whose main activity is providing full board and lodging facilities for visitors. Please do not assume that a so-called "inn" has guest bedrooms, or that a "pub" has not. There is considerable overlap. If you are thinking of staying overnight it is obviously sensible to write or phone for full details. Most inns which offer accommodation produce a proper brochure, which they will be pleased to send you.

Whilst many of the inns described here offer very attractive accommodation at reasonable prices, it is worth bearing in mind that any place which has a substantial pub trade is likely to be busy, and perhaps noisy, until late in the evening. This is particularly true of Fridays and Saturdays – and any other evenings when there are special activities or attractions such as live music.

THE STAR-RATING SYSTEM

I have used a Star-Rating system for various important items, including Comfort, Toilets, and Parking facilities. You will find the star-ratings on the same page as the photograph or drawing of each inn. As far as I am aware, they are a unique feature of this book. I have allocated the star-ratings myself, on the basis of personal observation. Please bear in mind that I have generally visited inns at lunchtime, often in the middle of the week. Ratings for items such as "Atmosphere" and "Cleanliness" might have been different had my visit been an evening one at the weekend!

The individual ratings vary between one-star (*) and four-star (****), the more stars the better. It's difficult to give a precise meaning to the various grades, but the following is about the best I can do:

*	adequate
**	fair-to-good
***	good-to-very-good
****	excellent

The individual items given star-ratings are discussed below.

FURNISHINGS

This rating refers to the quality of the furnishings, fittings, and decorations, principally in the lounge bar. My personal preference is for antique furniture in an "old pub" atmosphere, so a **** rating is likely to denote some good antique items, attractive pictures or prints, and thoughtful fabrics, in a decorative scheme which shows real signs of care. Needless to say such excellence is not often attained. Please note that a high score for furnishings does not necessarily imply a high level of comfort, which is assessed separately.

COMFORT

This applies to the comfort of seating, mainly in the lounge bar. A **** rating implies at least some really comfortable chairs or sofas, and decently covered additional seating. A * star rating probably means hard wooden chairs, benches, or unforgiving settles.

ATMOSPHERE

I'm not sure that it is wise to attempt a rating for this most fickle of attributes, but I wanted to give some idea of the welcome given to strangers, the courtesy of the staff, and the general human atmosphere. Almost all the inns listed here, being in my view delightful, score highly on this point.

GARDEN

The garden rating also applies to any outside area such as a terrace. A **** garden is likely to be very attractive, well-maintained, and generous in size with good garden furniture. A * star rating signifies a small outside area which hardly adds anything to the inn's facilities – or maybe a rather larger one which is poorly kept.

VIEWS

A high rating means that the inn or pub is very attractively situated, with good views of the surrounding countryside from its garden or outside area. A **** rating implies exceptional views – typically over fine countryside, a river estuary, or the sea. Many inns in villages, with a pleasant but rather restricted outlook, merit a ** rating. Please bear in mind that the views assessed are those from the outside of the building; it is generally not possible to enjoy them from within.

"OFF THE BEATEN TRACK" (OBT)

Since this book is about inns and pubs which are away from towns, cities, and main roads, I thought it would be a good idea to include an "Off the Beaten Track" rating. I have given a * star rating to any place which is on a B-category road, and therefore likely to attract a fair amount of passing traffic. My ** and *** star ratings relate to places increasingly away from the crowds. If you really want to find an inn in deep countryside (probably requiring map-reading skills and a certain amount of dogged determination), then aim for one with a **** rating. Do however bear in mind that it may be well known to the locals, and is not necessarily unfrequented.

CLEANLINESS

In allocating stars for cleanliness, I accept that this aspect of an inn can vary from day to day, and may not have been typical on my visit. Nevertheless some places are clearly so spotless that they merit a **** rating, whereas others are less diligently maintained. The cleanliness rating relates to bars and outside areas – but not to kitchens, accommodation, or loos.

TOILETS

I confess that, for obvious reasons, I have generally only obtained information on the Gents' loos! However, judging by those occasions when I have had the benefit of female advice, it seems that the facilities for Ladies are usually of comparable standard. A **** loo is a veritable delight, probably carpeted, certainly sweet and welcoming, with modern facilities. At the other end of the scale, a * model is of the basic variety, often semi-outside and draughty – the sort of place one gets into and out of as fast as nature permits.

PARKING

This rating tries to assess the ease and convenience with which you will be able to park your car on arrival. It relates not only to the number of parking spaces, but also to the inn's popularity. Thus a well-known inn in tourist country, not far from main roads or a town, may need 60 or 70 well laid-out parking spaces to merit a **** rating. One thoroughly off the beaten track may need only 15 or 20. If I have allocated * for parking, you should expect some difficulty if you arrive at any but the slackest of times.

1
FLEECE INN

Hillesley, Avon

Whitbread

Telephone: (0453) 843189
Open: 11-2.30; 6.30-10.30
Lunchtime and evening meals and snacks
Beers: Flowers; Guest beers
Garden suitable for children
Accommodation

Furnishings:	**	Garden:	***	Cleanliness:	**
Comfort:	**	Views:	**	Toilets:	*
Atmosphere:	***	OBT:	**	Parking:	***

If you were to ask 20 residents of the county of Avon to direct you to Hillesley, I guarantee that 19 of them would look entirely blank. It is quite a substantial village – but by English standards it is decidedly off the beaten track. With many of the characteristics of the Cotswolds, but well away from the tourist beat, Hillesley has a calm and charm of its own. I hasten to add that it is not beautiful in the picture-postcard sense, and I doubt (although I do not know for sure) whether it has buildings of special merit. No, the attraction of Hillesley is that it feels like rural England a generation ago, and there seems a fair chance that this situation will continue.

Approaching Hillesley from the A46, via Hawkesbury Upton, you get superb views over the countryside to the west as you wind down over the Cotswold scarp and into the village.

The Fleece Inn is, like its surroundings, neither especially elegant nor self-aware. It is, quite simply, its own place. The pub's appeal, to me at any rate, is diffuse and has more to do with its situation in an English village than with the details of furniture or facilities. In the small but reasonably comfortable lounge bar, you are free to tuck yourself away in a corner with a newspaper; or you may, likely as not, engage some local people in friendly conversation and learn a thing or two about Hillesley and the World.

The outside of the Fleece is particularly attractive and owes much to the Cotswold style. It has the traditional roof – small stone tiles at the top, continuously graded to larger ones at the bottom. The weight must be enormous. If you have the chance, visit the Fleece on a warm summer's day when you can sit outside. Then you can survey not only the building, but also a pleasant garden, a delightful Cotswold barn, and some exotic birds kept by the owners. If you have young children with you, there is a separate play area with an unusual facility – a rather splendid climbing apparatus constructed from old wooden beer barrels, complete with a miniature thatched roof in the form of a dovecote.

There is quite a good car park for about 20 cars, and access for a wheelchair seems reasonable, both to the garden and the front door of the pub (but not alas the loos!).

HOW TO GET THERE: Hillesley is about 17 miles north-east of Bristol. Turn off the A46 at Dunkirk (about 6 miles north of its junction with the M4, and 200 yards south of its junction with the A433), into a small road called France Lane, signposted to Hawkesbury Upton and Hillesley. Pass through Hawkesbury Upton, following signs for Hillesley. The inn is near the centre of the village, on the right hand side.

O.S. sheet 172, ref: 770897

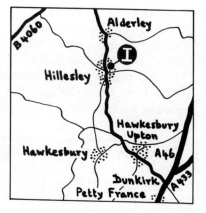

2
ANCHOR INN

Oldbury on Severn, Avon

Free House

Telephone: (0454) 413331
Open: 11.30-2.30; 6.30-10.30 (Fri, Sat 6.30-11)
Lunchtime and evening meals and snacks
*Beers** Butcombe Bitter; Marston Pedigree;
      Draught Bass; Theakston Best Bitter
Wine List; Wines by the glass
Garden suitable for children

Furnishings:	★★★	Garden:	★★★	Cleanliness:	★★★★
Comfort:	★★★	Views:	★★	Toilets:	★★★★
Atmosphere:	★★★★	OBT:	★★	Parking:	★★

You should have little difficulty in finding Oldbury on Severn, a substantial village some 12 miles north of Bristol and 3 miles west of Thornbury. Once there, the Anchor Inn is easily located. For one thing, it lies on the circular road through the village, beside a small bridge; and for another, the pub is very well known to the locals.

Apart from the resident nuclear power station, which is hardly visible from the village, Oldbury is a delightful spot. Very rural, well removed from the standard tourist beat, there is little reason for coming here unless you really mean it. This is flat country close to the Severn estuary, and Oldbury's St. Arilda church, perched for centuries on its little tumulus, offers marvellous views of the surrounding countryside.

A pub as well known, and widely praised, as the Anchor Inn is in mortal danger on at least two counts. It must resist the urge to expand; and it must avoid complacency. In such matters the Anchor strikes me as admirable. True, it has grown somewhat by adding a restaurant at the back; but this is well in keeping with the original building. And its staff remain courteous, friendly, and determined to make one feel at home.

The main bar of the pub is a single large room, simply and attractively furnished, with a superb open fireplace. The seating is good and comfortable – especially if you arrive early enough to claim one of the armchairs. The bar is on several levels, with steps between. The overall impression is of a very well run establishment which strikes a nice balance between old-fashioned charm and modern amenity. The loos, for example, are excellent; indeed, they verge on the luxurious.

The pub building is unexceptional outside, but there is a very good garden with a flat well-kept lawn, small trees, dovecote, and wooden furniture. A stream, draining the surrounding land into the estuary, runs alongside, and there are occasional glimpses of the distant hills of Monmouth. There is good level access for a wheelchair from the car park to the garden, or, via a side-door, to the loos, restaurant, and one of the levels of the main bar. Car parking at the front of the pub caters for about 12 cars, with a similar number outside on the lane. This is by no means overgenerous.

As you will have gathered, I find it hard to fault the Anchor Inn. Especially commendable is its ability to shrug off fame and preserve its character. Long may it hold firm.

HOW TO GET THERE: Approach via the A38 and B4061, taking a minor road to Oldbury from the northern outskirts of Thornbury. As you near Oldbury, avoid the Power Station road, and wind your way through the main part of the village. This involves a sharp left turn into Church Road, after which you will soon see the pub on your left.

O.S. sheet 172, ref: 609924

3
FOX INN
Old Down, Avon

Free House

Telephone: (0454) 412507
Open: 11-2.30; 6-10.30 (Fri, Sat 6-11)
Lunchtime meals and snacks; Evening snacks
*Beers** Davenports Bitter; Draught Bass; Flowers IPA
Wines by the glass
Garden suitable for children

Furnishings:	**	Garden:	****	Cleanliness:	****
Comfort:	***	Views:	**	Toilets:	****
Atmosphere:	***	OBT:	***	Parking:	***

Old Down is quite close to Bristol, and even closer to the M4-M5 motorway junction at Almondsbury. In spirit and in character, however, it seems 100 miles from both. The Fox Inn is tucked away in a village backwater and cleverly concealed from view. It is hardly a pub you would stumble across, and presumably attracts very little casual passing trade. I regard it more as the fruit of diligent research.

The Fox, although based on a 300-year-old building, has been substantially renovated and altered. This has obviously added to its comfort and convenience, although the interior is now rather less quaint than many old inns. There is a single, large, L-shaped main room, with very low beams, a wood-block floor, open fireplace, and quite comfortable seating. One of the pleasurable results of renovation is that the loos are excellent.

For me, the main recommendation of this pub is its very attractive garden, and an outside covered area which looks and feels like a verandah. Glass-topped, and extending round two sides of the stone building, it has tables and chairs for about 25 people, and harbours an extremely healthy-looking vine and some lovely floral hanging baskets, watered by a purpose-built sprinker system. The covered area is so well constructed that it should be possible to eat or drink outside, in some style, during a thunderstorm.

The garden is quite large and very sunny, with a fine Chestnut tree and plenty of flowers. There are wooden picnic tables on a carefully tended lawn, plus swings and a slide for children. A well-surfaced car park has space for about 30 cars, and there is good level access from it to the garden, and to the pub (via a few very low ridges or steps). Since the pub is on level ground there are no distant views, but the setting is both peaceful and rural. On my most recent visit in early autumn, the vine had a marvellous load of black grapes which were about to be turned into wine by a local enthusiast.

The Fox shows every sign of being expertly and efficiently run. If these twin virtues detract slightly from the notion of old-fashioned charm, then so be it. Very few pubs offer such an attractive and unusual outdoor setting within a few miles of a great city.

HOW TO GET THERE: From the straggling village of Rudgeway on the A38 about 8 miles north of Bristol, take a well-signposted turning to Lower Hazel and Old Down. You will come to Old Down after about a mile and a half. As you enter the village there is a public telephone on your left. Turn left immediately before it into a lane called The Inner Down, where the Fox is situated.

O.S. sheet 172, ref: 618874

4
BLACK HORSE

Clapton in Gordano, Avon

Courage

Telephone: (0272) 842105
Open: 11-2.30 (Sun 12-2.30); 6-11 (Sun 7-10.30)
Lunchtime meals (not Sundays); snacks
Beers: Courage Best Bitter; Courage Bitter Ale
Family room; Garden suitable for children
Dogs allowed in garden; and on lead in bars

Furnishings:	★★★	Garden:	★★	Cleanliness:	★★
Comfort:	★★	Views:	★★	Toilets:	★★
Atmosphere:	★★★	OBT:	★★★	Parking:	★★★★

The small village of Clapton in Gordano is about 7 miles west of Bristol, and, for the uninitiated, is probably best approached from the Bristol-Clevedon road, B3128. The village lies at one side of the attractive Gordano valley, now somewhat compromised by the M5 motorway. However, even though the motorway runs within 200 yards of the village, it is mercifully hidden from sight and sound by an intervening hillside, and there are no easy access points. This makes Clapton a surprisingly peaceful spot.

The venerable Black Horse is said to have stood here for more than 600 years. It nestles comfortably in the middle of the village, on the ancient way between Bristol, Portbury, and Clevedon. This is really a classic West Country pub, with stone floors and simple furniture. In the 20 years since my first visit it has changed very little, and, as far as I can tell, it has very little intention of changing in the future.

There are three main rooms – a fairly rough one with a billiard table, a large stone-flagged one with an open fire and simple seating, and a cosy inner bar with a wealth of local pictures, photos, mugs, and mementos. There is some danger here of inundation by knick-knacks, but at least they are of the genuine, non-brassy, kind. Although the inner bar is the most comfortable, with a variety of cushioned seats and settles, it is hardly luxurious – but it has considerable atmosphere. I should add that, since it has tiny windows let into massive walls, it is very dark. The pub boasts four or five old wall clocks, none of which appears to have any connection whatsoever with electricity or quartz.

Car parking is unusually good for a country pub – a large, well-surfaced area at the back with space for about 40 cars. There is level access for a wheelchair from the park to a back door. At the far end of the car park, next to a yard with a few hens scratching around, is a pleasant small garden area with wooden picnic tables, two swings, and a childrens' wooden climbing frame. There is also a very small front garden.

The Black Horse is by no means super-smart or brightly scrubbed, nor are its individual features particularly unusual. But there is a very good atmosphere here, and a great feeling of continuity in a rural setting – especially when one remembers just how close it is to Bristol and the docks at Portbury and Avonmouth.

HOW TO GET THERE: Clapton in Gordano is well signposted (as "Clapton") from the Bristol-Clevedon road, B3128. You enter the village down a steep hill, with a sharp left turn at the bottom, followed by a sharp right. 50 yards further on, turn left into Clevedon Lane. The pub is 200 yards up the lane.

If you enter Clapton from the Portishead direction, turn right into Clevedon Lane about 50 yards past the bus shelter.

O.S. sheet 172, ref: 473739

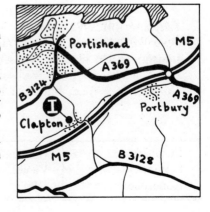

5
BULL
Hinton, Avon

Wadworth

Telephone: (027 582) 2332
Open: 10.30-2.30; 6.30-10.30 (Fri, Sat 6.30-11)
Lunchtime and evening meals and snacks
Beers★ Wadworth IPA; Wadworth 6X
No dogs in garden, but ideal for children

Furnishings:	★★★	Garden:	★★★★	Cleanliness:	★★
Comfort:	★★	Views:	★★★	Toilets:	★★★
Atmosphere:	★★★	OBT:	★★★	Parking:	★★★★

The Bull at Hinton stands, as its name implies, four-square in its country setting. Even the inn-sign, a majestically painted animal without name or embellishment, suggests a solid permanence. If you come to the Bull from the frenzy of the M4 motorway, which lies about a mile to the north, you will no doubt relish the contrast.

Hinton is a very small village with a telephone and a pub, and not a great deal besides. It lies adjacent to the National Trust house at Dyrham, whose park, originally laid out in the 1690's as a Dutch water garden, was later converted to the less formal English landscape style. Apart from the constant slight drone of traffic on the motorway (which is just visible from the pub garden), this is a delightfully peaceful spot.

The Bull is on the outskirts of the village, and faces fields and woodland. To one side it has a fine open garden – one the the largest pub gardens I have seen. When I went there in May there was little evidence of garden furniture, apart from a few rather tatty wooden seats and tables; but the open prospect, giving fine views to the west and north, was a real tonic. The garden is perhaps better described as a meadow, allowing children a lovely romp without the risk of dog-mess – always assuming that the "No Dogs in Garden" sign means exactly what it says! Incidentally there is also a small paved area at the front of the pub, overlooking the car park, with a few tables, benches, and chairs.

The interior is attractive and has a comfortable woody feeling about it. There is a large bar on the right, with plenty of tables, chairs and settles, some with cushions. On the left is a smaller, more comfortable, lounge bar leading to a restaurant. Overall, the impression is of a homely place where it would be a pleasure to rest after a long walk, a cycle ride, or a car journey.

There is a very good car park for about 30 vehicles at the front of the building. Access for a wheelchair is reasonable to the garden (apart from the slope), and possibly also into the pub via a side entrance. However the front entrance is guarded by some high steps. The loos inside the building are very good; there are some other ones outside, for those using the garden.

I have very few criticisms to make of this lovely pub. About the only things that come to mind are the slight tattiness of the garden furniture, and minor evidence of litter at the front. These may well be transient problems.

HOW TO GET THERE: Hinton is about 10 miles east of Bristol, and just south of the M4 Motorway. It is clearly signposted from the A46 about three quarters of a mile south of its junction with the M4. The turning is opposite a pub called the Crown Inn. Following the lane down into Hinton, you will see the Bull on your right after about a mile, just before entering the village proper.

O.S. sheet 172, ref: 737768

6
DRUIDS ARMS
Stanton Drew, Avon

Courage

Telephone: (0272) 332230
Open: 11.30-2.30 (Sun 12-2.30); 6-11 (Sun 7-10.30)
Lunchtime and evening snacks
Beers: Courage Best Bitter; Courage Directors;
      John Smiths Yorkshire Bitter
Wines by the glass
Garden and terrace suitable for children
Dogs admitted

Furnishings:	★★	Garden:	★★★	Cleanliness:	★★★
Comfort:	★★	Views:	★★★	Toilets:	★★
Atmosphere:	★★★	OBT:	★★★	Parking:	★★★

You have at least two good excuses for visiting Stanton Drew, and you will no doubt think of some way of combining them. In no particular order, there is the attractive Druids Arms; and there are some famous stone circles which have stood here for about four thousand years, giving this small Avon village a rather special character.

Romantics may be disappointed to learn that Stanton Drew has no connection with the Druids. It gets its name from the Drew family, who seem to have made a hobby of collecting estates with megaliths in them during the Middle Ages (Drewsteignton in Devon, Littleton Drew in Wiltshire). The pub can therefore be accused of trading under a misnomer, and its highly imaginative inn sign compounds the felony!

The stones of Stanton Drew comprise a great circle nearly a quarter of a mile around, two much smaller circles, and the famous Cove or arch with its two standing stones and one fallen one. Although various theories have linked them with worship of the sun, moon, and planets, local tradition has it that the stones are the remains of a wedding party, petrified for extending revelries beyond Saturday night into Sunday morning. Maybe this explains why, in Stanton Drew, the call "Time Gentlemen, Please" can assume a certain urgency.

The Druids Arms is a fairly small stone-built pub fronting directly onto the lane, and overlooking meadows. There are some picnic tables outside – rather too close to the road for comfort, but at least there is very little passing traffic. A wheelchair user will find a 5-inch step at the front door. The pub has a very good raised back garden, within arm's reach of the Cove, and I understand it has recently been opened up to guests. There is good parking for about 20 cars, plus another 25 or so in a rougher, overspill, park.

The inside has two smallish bars. The one on the right has a fruit machine and leads into a further area with darts board and jukebox. The lounge on the left is the more attractively furnished and decorated, and should be relatively immune from electronic noise. Seating is reasonably soft and comfortable. I confess that the inside of the Druids Arms does not quite live up to the very attractive village setting, and I was offered a limited range of lunchtime snacks, with no frills. On the other hand I much enjoyed the unpretentious, friendly, local atmosphere.

HOW TO GET THERE: Stanton Drew is about 6 miles south of Bristol as the crow flies. Take the B3130 from its junction with the A37, towards Chew Magna. Turn left to Stanton Drew after about a mile and a half, alongside a quaint thatched cottage standing alone on a little traffic island. Wind your way through the village, following signs for the Cove, and you will find the pub at the far end on your left.

O.S. sheet 172, ref: 597632

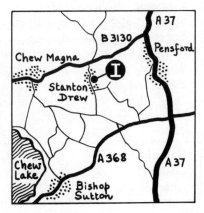

7
PONY AND TRAP
Newtown, Chew Magna, Avon

Courage

Telephone: (0272) 332627
Open: 12-3; 6-11 (Sun 7-10.30)
Lunchtime snacks only
Beers: Courage Best Bitter; Courage Bitter Ale
Wines by the glass
Family room; Garden suitable for children
Dogs allowed in bars and garden, on lead only

Furnishings:	★★★	Garden:	★★	Cleanliness:	★★
Comfort:	★★★	Views:	★★★★	Toilets:	★
Atmosphere:	★★★	OBT:	★★★★	Parking:	★★★

The Pony and Trap has a delightful rural setting, and yet it is only 4 miles as the crow flies from the urban sprawl of southern Bristol. The reason is not hard to explain. Between the two rises the long shoulder of Dundry Hill, which effectively isolates the city from its rural hinterland. And it is this hill which acts as guardian of the pub's tranquility.

Try to visit the Pony and Trap on a bright clear day when clouds scud in from the south west, playing dappled forms upon the slopes of Dundry and the intervening landscape. Then look closer, at the field behind the pub where the geese hold court, and you should feel a very long way from city cares.

The old stone building is quite small, although it has been added to at the back. A fine front door leads directly into the main bar which is attractively furnished in traditional style. Benches and chairs are comfortably upholstered, even though some of them are a little rickety. The overall feel of this bar is very cosy and welcoming – just the sort of place to spend an hour or two in cold midwinter. However I feel I should warn you that the pub has a restricted choice of lunchtime snacks, and you are unlikely to be offered much more than sandwiches or a ploughman's lunch. No food is served in the evenings. Leading off the main bar, and down a few steps, are several small rooms, including a family room. All have the fine views towards Dundry. Weather permitting, you can go out onto a small paved garden area with wooden seating – some of which appears to have started life in a church – and experience goose-talk at closer quarters. You will also see an old bath pressed into service as a very large flower pot, and set rather cheekily into a wall.

Motorists will be pleased to find a well-surfaced car park at the side of the pub. This is just as well, because the lane outside is very narrow. Unfortunately the Pony and Trap is not really suitable for wheelchairs; there are quite high steps at both the main door and the side entrance.

The Pony and Trap is certainly off the beaten track. Newtown, the hamlet which contains it, consists of a few cottages spread along the lane. So please do not expect to find the glitter and sophistication of a well-known pub in tourist country; the attractions here are of another kind.

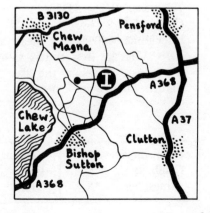

HOW TO GET THERE: Take the B3130 to Chew Magna, about 7 miles south of Bristol. Turn off in the centre of the village, alongside the Pelican Inn. The road is signposted (not very clearly!) to Bishop Sutton and Bath. Follow its twists and turns for just over a mile, latterly up a long hill between hedgerows, and you will find the pub near the top on your left.

O.S. sheet 172, ref: 588613

29

8
WHEATSHEAF
Combe Hay, Avon

Courage

Telephone: (0225) 833504
Open: 11-11
Lunchtime and evening meals and snacks
Beers: Courage Best Bitter; Courage Directors
Wine List; Wines by the glass
Garden suitable for children

Furnishings:	★★★	Garden:	★★★	Cleanliness:	★★★
Comfort:	★★	Views:	★★★★	Toilets:	★★
Atmosphere:	★★	OBT:	★★★	Parking:	★★★

The landscape south of Bath is riven with steeply-wooded combes, many of which shelter a stone-built village. Road access is often tortuous. Yet the effort is amply rewarded, for this is rural England at its most intimate. In one such valley, just three or four miles from Bath and well off the beaten track, lies the Wheatsheaf at Combe Hay.

You enter Combe Hay down a twisting lane past cottages and fine houses of honey-coloured stone. The pub is at the far end of the village, set against a hillside. If you come by car you will need a modicum of skill to reach the car park, which has about the steepest entry of any I have seen. All this accomplished, you will probably need rest and revictualling. I doubt if the Wheatsheaf will disappoint you.

The inside of the pub contains a large lounge bar made up of three interconnected rooms. The bar itself is at the back, in a rather dark corner. At the front are two cosier, carpeted, areas, with low-beamed ceilings and a large open fireplace. There is also a medium size restaurant. The furnishings are attractively unfussy, with a variety of wooden seating including modern Windsor-style chairs (but no cushions!). Chalked up on a large wallboard, in traditional style, is an extensive menu of hot and cold snacks and meals.

The Wheatsheaf is quite a large pub, which strikes me as rather less intimate than the rest of Combe Hay. It gives the feeling of a popular local enterprise, with a solid trade. I do not blame it for this – I merely point it out, so that you will not come expecting a higgledy-piggledy building frequented by country bumpkins.

Unusually, the garden is entirely at the front of the pub; happily, it is also well away from the car park. It has lovely views over the wooded valley, without a building in sight. The garden furniture, especially the seating, is rather more decorative than comfortable, and could do with a little attention. But the overall effect is charming, and the barbecue in one corner of the garden suggests some enjoyable summer evenings in the green. I should also mention the three dovecotes let into the stonework of the building, which show emphatic signs of multiple occupation.

There is good car parking for about 50 cars, on three levels. Wheelchair access is made difficult by slopes and steps, unless you are early enough to get a place in the lower car park, and content to stay in the garden.

HOW TO GET THERE: Take the A367 out of Bath towards Radstock. About 3 miles from the centre of Bath, you will see a pub called Crossways House on the right of the main road, in open country. At this point turn sharp left into a narrow lane signposted to Combe Hay. You will come to a crossroads after about a mile. The village of Combe Hay is straight ahead, and the pub is at its far end.

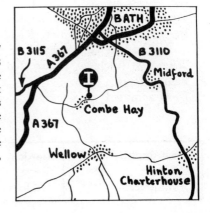

O.S. sheet 172, ref: 736600

31

9
FOX AND BADGER
Wellow, Avon

Ushers

Telephone: (0225) 832293
Open: 11-2.30 (Sat, Sun 11-3); 6.30-11
Meals and snacks whenever the pub is open
Beers: Ushers Best Bitter; Ruddles Best Bitter;
        Draught Guinness; Holsten Lager
Wine List (includes House Red & White); Wines by the glass
Family room
Dogs admitted

Furnishings:	★★★★	Garden:	★★	Cleanliness:	★★
Comfort:	★★	Views:	★	Toilets:	★★
Atmosphere:	★★★★	OBT:	★★	Parking:	★

If you tire of the bustle of Bath, try dropping down to Wellow. It is the sort of place that city dwellers dream about - neither rich nor poor, neither swish nor drab, but simply a village where a few hundred live surrounded by mellow stone, and time stands relatively still.

You can hardly miss the Fox and Badger, which is at the village centre. Its outside paintwork may be a little faded, but the delicious inn sign promises a pub of character. Inside you will find two bars. I suppose that the one on the left could fairly be described as rugged (you must cross it if you need the loo!). The lounge on the right is just what I hope to find in a pub which has been going for a very long time, and clearly intends to continue. Its age is palpable – a fine mixture of huge-flagged floor, stone walls, wooden furniture, an old piano, and a fireplace bearing signs of centuries of smoke. The seating has been brightly, recently, and comfortably upholstered. So although the room is a little dark, it is far from dingy. There is Shove Ha'Penny, and a skittle alley.

The Fox and Badger feels like a home as well as a pub, and there is evidence of home cooking. Out at the back past the family room, you will find a small paved yard with flowers, vines, and some middle-aged wooden furniture. There could also be a line of washing. The yard is so sheltered by high walls that a drink out here in March or October must often prove a pleasure.

Car drivers should, with luck, be able to park in the street nearby. There is level access for a wheelchair, although I suspect the doorway itself might prove a little narrow.

Opposite the pub a signpost announces, quite correctly, that one arm of a crossroads leads to Hinton Charterhouse, another to Twinhoe. But even those familiar with the convolutions of English place names will find the third one hard to stomach: Caution Deep Ford. In fairness I admit that the message has at some stage been painted over, presumably in embarrassment.

There is a point to this story. I want to encourage you to try the lane to Caution Deep Ford (on foot, emphatically not by car). Within two or three hundred steep yards you will see some stone cottages with lovely gardens, an old packhorse bridge, maybe a trout or a kingfisher, and a threat of drowning to a depth of 6 feet. As you climb back to the Fox and Badger, past the bridge stonework that used to carry steam trains from Bath to Radstock, you will probably feel a bit in love with Wellow.

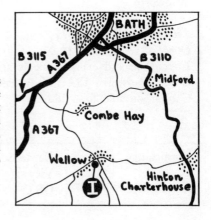

HOW TO GET THERE: Wellow is about 4 miles south of Bath. Take the A367 from Bath towards Radstock. About 5 miles out of Bath, turn left at the far end of the village of Peasedown St. John, alongside the Red Post Inn. You will reach Wellow after two miles, and the pub is at its centre.

O.S. sheet 172, ref: 740583

10
NEW INN
Blagdon, Avon

Wadworth

Telephone: (0761) 62475
Open: 11-2.30; 6.30-10.30
Lunchtime and evening meals and snacks
Beers: Wadworth IPA; Wadworth 6X
Garden suitable for children

Furnishings:	★★★	Garden:	★★	Cleanliness:	★★★
Comfort:	★★★	Views:	★★★★	Toilets:	★★★
Atmosphere:	★★★	OBT:	★★	Parking:	★★★★

Under the northern slopes of the Mendip Hills lies Blagdon, well known as an attractive village within easy reach of Bristol. The New Inn (which, like all the best New Inns, is as old as Adam) is tucked away down by the church, well clear of the main road and close to Blagdon Lake.

The New Inn is a delight for two main reasons. Firstly, it has a splendid situation overlooking the lake, with a decent garden. Secondly, it has a very friendly atmosphere, and seems to offer good food. When I was there I enjoyed some excellent homemade steak and kidney pie, plus jacket potato and salad. The comprehensive menu and reasonable prices must appeal to the locals too, because they were there in considerable numbers.

Inside, the main bar is a generous lounge on two levels, with wooden tables and a mixture of chairs, armchairs, stools, and benches – many of them comfortably upholstered in red. There is a large open fireplace, plenty of dark woodwork, and some attractive brass and copper. The overall feeling is traditional and calm. This is the type of place that gives English pubs their reputation for civilised drinking and conversation, away from the immediate troubles of the World.

As I have said, the exterior of this pub is exceptional. The building itself is attractive and well maintained. There is a good garden at the back, with a superb outlook over the lake. It is, perhaps, a little too close to the car park for proper peace and quiet – but then this is the ransom we pay to King Car. The garden furniture is a mixture of wooden picnic tables and rather more substantial tables with cast iron bases, some of them pitched on rather sloping ground. I can imagine difficulty maintaining the equilibrium of a pint of bitter here - let alone an avocado pear. But the overall situation of the New Inn is unusually delightful.

If you stroll, or roll, down the very steep lane outside the pub, you will come after half a mile to the head of Blagdon Lake and can walk across the dam. The lake is a reservoir for Bristol and the surrounding area. Here you will very likely see a variety of wintering water birds in the colder months, or fly fishermen in the warmer ones.

Car parking is very good with space for about 55 cars. Wheelchair access to the garden is easy, and to the pub reasonable if you can negotiate a few very low steps or ridges.

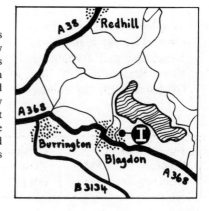

HOW TO GET THERE: Blagdon is about 10 miles south of Bristol as the crow flies, and straddles the A368. The inn is close to the church, between the main road and the lake. Turn off the main road into narrow Church Street, immediately opposite a pub called The Live and Let Live. Proceed gently down through the village for about a quarter of a mile, and you will find the inn on your right just as the lake comes into view.

O.S. sheet 172, ref: 505589

11
WHEATSHEAF INN

Stone Allerton, Somerset

Free House

Telephone: (0934) 712494
Open: 12-2.30; 6-10.30
Lunchtime and evening meals and snacks
Beers: Real Ales
Garden suitable for children

Furnishings:	★★★	Garden:	★★★	Cleanliness:	★★★★
Comfort:	★★★	Views:	★★	Toilets:	★★
Atmosphere:	★★★★	OBT:	★★★	Parking:	★★★★

I doubt if most residents of Somerset know the whereabouts of Stone Allerton, even though it lies within a dozen miles of Wells, Cheddar, and Weston super Mare. Together with its close cousin Chapel Allerton, it sits comfortably above the surrounding Levels on the firm, fertile, ground of the isle of Wedmore. And if, after sampling the delights of the Wheatsheaf Inn, you have an hour or two to spare, you could do a great deal worse than visit Wedmore, one of the most appealing of Somerset villages, with fine houses and a civilised air. It is hard today to understand how Hannah More, 19th century educational reformer and high-churchwoman, could have experienced such special difficulty in setting up a school in "depraved and shocking" Wedmore against the wishes of its brutalised farmers.

The Wheatsheaf is an unusually delightful pub, set sideways on the lane, with an attractive garden at one side – complete with genuine well – and a first-class car park at the other. The pub is on level ground, and wheelchair access looks straightforward. Since I am about to lavish fulsome praise on the inside of the pub, I can perhaps mention the loos, which are along a path towards the back, a little draughty, and slightly less admirable than the rest of the facilities.

The inside offers more or less everything I hope to find in a delightful country pub: small enough to feel intimate, with courteous and attentive staff; comfortably and tastefully furnished without a jumble of knick-knacks; and with soft lighting to enhance the already cosy atmosphere. The lounge bar has a low ceiling with single beam, and is generally painted cream apart from the natural stone wall and fireplace at the far end, with cushioned wooden chairs and benches. There are some interesting pictures and prints, and a number of elaborate corn dollies which I gather are locally made. Leading off the lounge bar, small and a little cavernous, is an eating area with just four or five tables. I suppose the whole place would seem distinctly full with 25 or 30 people. Fortunately there is also a public bar further along the slender frontage of the building, and this too looks attractive and welcoming.

Appearing several times on the inn's walls, and in reality just half a mile down the lane, stands the last traditional windmill to be worked in Somerset. With fine stone tower and wooden cap, Ashton Mill still commands wonderful views in the direction of the prevailing wind.

HOW TO GET THERE: Stone Allerton lies about a mile and a half west of the A38, and 2 or 3 miles south of Axbridge and the Mendip ridge.

Travelling south on the A38, turn left in Lower Weare along a lane signposted to Weare, Chapel Allerton, and Wedmore. Bear right after half a mile to the Allertons, and continue for another mile and a half past quite a number of houses. The pub is on the right-hand side towards the far end of the village.

O.S. sheet 182, ref: 408510

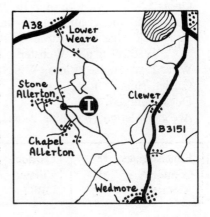

12
NEW INN

Priddy, Somerset

Free House

Telephone: (0749) 76465
Open: 12-2.30; 7-11 (Sun 7-10.30)
Lunchtime and evening meals and snacks
Beers* Eldridge Pope Royal Oak; Marston Pedigree;
      Wadworth 6X; Websters Yorkshire Bitter
Wine List; House Wines; Wine by the glass
Garden suitable for children
Dogs admitted
Accommodation (5 double rooms, 1 family room)

Furnishings:	★★★	Garden:	★★★	Cleanliness:	★★
Comfort:	★★	Views:	★★	Toilets:	★★
Atmosphere:	★★★	OBT:	★★★	Parking:	★★★

In the middle of the village green at Priddy, within view of the New Inn, stands a small thatched edifice which can easily be mistaken at first sight for a barn. But it turns out to be a huge stack of sheep hurdles, awaiting yet another of Priddy's August sheep fairs – a major local event which has been held here since the village took it over from plague-ridden Wells in 1348.

Priddy is high on the Mendip plateau, a little bleak and windswept, but with plenty of its own character. It was formerly a lead-mining village, whose hard living was wrung from the ground well within living memory. You will not find the soft breezes of the southern slopes round Cheddar, scented with strawberries and flowers. No, it is altogether more rugged country, and the village green is hardly the cosy place of tourist guide books – without gentrified country cottages, Olde Worlde tea shops, or floral displays. The green at Priddy is large but fairly empty, with some fine farm buildings, the stack of hurdles, a few houses, and the New Inn.

The pub has plenty of character too, especially inside. The lounge bar is split in two by a robust stone archway and stone-arched window. There is a good carpet, lots of quite comfortable upholstered benches, and wooden chairs. The inner part of the bar is very attractive in a rugged way, with a superb old fireplace, some good brass ornaments, and more padded benches. It's a little dark, and unpretentious, but with a character which seems just right for Priddy. There is also a restaurant towards the back.

Going from the bars to the garden, you will pass through a long slender porch with a couple of extra tables. In warm weather there is a welcoming front terrace looking out over the green, and a generous side garden with picnic tables and some diversions for children. Car parking is also quite generous – 8 or ten spaces immediately in front of the pub, another 15 or so in a car park at the side, and plenty of additional space around Priddy's green. Wheelchair access looks uncomplicated.

Apart from its lead-mining and Sheep Fair, Priddy is famous for an abundance of prehistoric circles, tumuli, and long barrows. One glance at an Ordnance Survey map will show you just how many there are. So after a pleasant hour or two in the New Inn, I suggest a walk up to North Hill, which gives an excellent feel for the special character of the high Mendips.

HOW TO GET THERE: Priddy is about 4 miles north-west of Wells. A good route is to take the minor road signposted to Priddy from the A39 about 3 miles north of Wells. The road is about 3 miles long, and straight. The inn is on the left hand side at the near end of the village green.

Priddy can also be reached from the B3135 between Cheddar and Shepton Mallet, being about 5 miles west of Cheddar.

O.S. sheet 183, ref: 527508

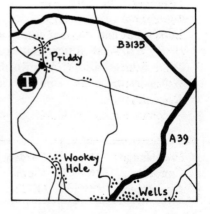

13
WHITE HART

Trudoxhill, Somerset

Free House

Telephone: (037 384) 324
Open: 12-2.30 (Sat 11.30-2.30); 7-11
Lunchtime and evening meals and snacks
Beers* Ash Vine Bitter; Butcombe Bitter;
      Adnams Bitter; Wadworth 6X
Wines by the glass; Draught cider

Furnishings:	★★★	Garden:	★★★	Cleanliness:	★★★
Comfort:	★★★	Views:	★★	Toilets:	★★
Atmosphere:	★★★	OBT:	★★	Parking:	★★★

The small village of Trudoxhill lies two or three miles from Frome, a fascinating old Somerset town which for centuries made its living by the manufacture of woollen cloth. Even nearer is the village of Nunney, with a famous 14th-century manor house crenellated like the Bastille. So if you decide to visit the White Hart, set in a hilly but rather unprepossessing village, there is plenty in the neighbourhood to fire your interest.

The White Hart is a fine old building in the grey local stone, with a red-tiled roof. To one side is a car park for about 25 cars, to the other an extremely attractive small garden with picnic tables set amongst a riot of flowers. Wheelchair access appears reasonable, with a single step at the front door – although the inner door might be a little awkward.

The pub's main bar stretches lengthwise across the building, and has an atmosphere which is both civilised and local. It's a place of dark wood, beamed ceilings, and stone, offset by an excellent reddish carpet and a refreshing lack of knick-knacks. The right-hand part of the bar extends back a little to provide some extra tables, and the seating is generally fairly comfortable with a mix of cushioned chairs and benches. This is a good, solid, unpretentious place with plenty of character.

Adjoining the garden towards the back of the pub is an outbuilding and – when I was there – a certain amount of junk. I hasten to add that it was being enthusiastically cleared in preparation for setting up a small brewery, the brainchild and creation of the present owner. I am not in the business of advertising, but it seems to me that in this age of Mega-breweries such initiatives deserve our full support. And it may be that by the time this book is published you will have, in little Trudoxhill, the chance to stretch out an arm from a delightful garden and tap an equally meritorious pint.

Apart from the White Hart, Trudoxhill's main claim to fame is a very early Congregational chapel, reflecting the strong Puritan tradition which had sent so many of the weavers of Frome, and miners of the Mendips, to join Monmouth's ragged rebellion of 1685. With graveyard and yew trees somehow suggesting the spirit of local nonconformity, the chapel's interior confirms the feeling with its tall pulpit, simple gallery, and plain pews. You will find it, dated 1699, a hundred yards down the side-lane from the pub, adjoining the village hall.

HOW TO GET THERE: Trudoxhill is about 3 miles south-west of Frome. Take the minor road signposted to the village from the A361, about 300 yards on the Frome side of the A361/A359 roundabout. You will come to the village after about a mile, and the pub is easily found on the left-hand side.

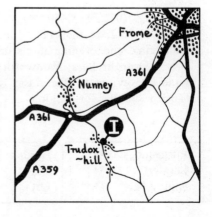

O.S. sheet 183, ref: 748438

14
STRODE ARMS

Cranmore, Somerset

Free House

Telephone: (074 988) 450
Open: 11.30-2.30; 6.30-11
Lunchtime and evening meals and snacks
Beers★ Draught Bass; Wadworth 6X
Wine list; Wines by the glass; Draught cider
Garden suitable for children

Furnishings:	★★★	Garden:	★★	Cleanliness:	★★★
Comfort:	★★★	Views:	★★	Toilets:	★★★
Atmosphere:	★★★★	OBT:	★★	Parking:	★★

If you happen to be enthusiastic about steam engines as well as pubs, the small village of Cranmore will present you with a double delight: not only is it home to the Strode Arms, but within a hundred and fifty yards you can explore the paraphernalia of the East Somerset Railway, brought back to life in 1975 after a long sleep. Cranmore lies just off the A361 two or three miles east of Shepton Mallet, and apart from its magnetism for connoisseurs of steam is well off the main West Country tourist routes.

The pub is built of the imposing local stone and has an attractive site overlooking the village duckpond, which is kept clean and tidy for its residents. There's a terrace with picnic tables at the front, and a small garden plus a car park for about 15 cars at the back. A further 8 or 10 vehicles can park at the front, beside the road. Wheelchair access seems reasonable onto the terrace, and into the pub via a double doorway.

You may feel that the greyness of the local stone gives the outside a slightly severe look, but the inside is undoubtedly welcoming. The main bar area, divided into three, is quite large, with a dark-beamed ceiling and walls which are a mix of natural stone and cream. There's some attractive brass and iron, an excellent open fireplace, pictures, and an old pine longcase clock. Seating is a mixture of wooden chairs, benches, padded stools and window seats, and there's a variety of wood-topped tables, some with wrought iron bases. Thoughtful and effective lighting gives the whole place a delightfully warm glow. On the right-hand side there is an attractive restaurant.

The East Somerset Railway, brainchild of the artist and wildlife campaigner David Shepherd, has its headquarters nearby at Cranmore station, and two or three miles of track – which I believe its enthusiasts are trying to extend. You don't have to be an expert to appreciate something of the magic of the steam engines, engine sheds, picturesque station buildings which include a cast-iron gents' ("please adjust your dress before leaving"), and the only signal box I know which doubles up as an art gallery. On a day when there were no engines in steam I was able to wander round the engine shed, marvelling at the scale of the Green Knight with its pistons and rods and gleaming paintwork. It must be a double thrill to see it on the move.

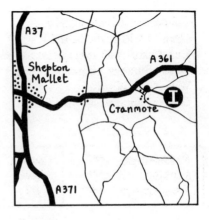

HOW TO GET THERE: Cranmore is signposted from the A361 about 3 miles east of Shepton Mallet. The pub is in a side lane near the centre of the village, almost opposite the entrance to the East Somerset Railway.

O.S. sheet 183, ref: 669433

15
OLD SHIP INN

Combwich, Somerset

Whitbread

Telephone: (0278) 652684
Open: 11.30-2.30; 6-10.30
Lunchtime and evening meals and snacks
Beers: Flowers Original; Flowers IPA
Wines by the glass
Garden suitable for children

Furnishings:	★★	Garden:	★★★	Cleanliness:	★★★
Comfort:	★★★	Views:	★★★	Toilets:	★★
Atmosphere:	★★★	OBT:	★★	Parking:	★★★

Combwich is where it is, and what it is, for being about 40 feet above mean sea level. This may sound no great height, but any Dutchman will confirm that when it comes to keeping dry – and safe – 40 feet can make a great deal of difference. The local importance of Combwich is (or was) that it occupies a small mound beside the widening river Parrett, midway between Bridgwater and the sea.

A century ago when the Severn estuary positively bristled with trading ships – coal from the South Wales ports, bricks and tiles from Bridgwater – the quays of Combwich were an important lifeline to the outside world. You can still sense this if you wander down to the river from the Old Ship Inn. There is, for example, a cast-iron notice dated 1898 and signed by one George Lovibond, threatening dire punishment to anyone "removing sand or shingle, or in any way interfering with or damaging the sea defences". The notice itself is in imminent danger of defacement, not by human agency but by the endless scouring of salt-laden winds. On a rather different tack, and far more poetically, one is forbidden to ride a horse on the cricket field which seems to have been sandwiched between the sea wall and the road.

The Old Ship is a fine building, recently redecorated inside and out. The medium size lounge bar is divided between some comfortable casual seating, and tables for those wishing to eat. The furnishings are new – or recently restored – and the decorations are unfussy. I cannot describe the interior as quaint, but it is pleasing, comfortable, and clean. At the back is a medium size garden on several levels, with lawn and paths and about a dozen picnic tables. Children clearly enjoy the swings, rope climber, and miniature house provided for their amusement – all apparently in good order. The garden looks out over an apple orchard complete with resident sheep. Although wheelchair access to the pub itself seems rather tricky because of some high steps, it is possible to get into the garden directly from the car park, via a little side gate. The car park is roughly-surfaced and sufficient for about 25 cars.

Combwich is a lovely spot, well off the tourist track, which will appeal to anyone who loves wide landscapes and big skies. I believe there are fine walks along the sea wall in both directions, and it is presumably possible to reach the Old Ship along the six miles of riverbank from Bridgwater.

HOW TO GET THERE: Combwich is about 4 miles north-west of Bridgwater. Take the A39 out of Bridgwater towards Minehead. After 3 miles turn right in the centre of the village of Cannington, alongside the agricultural college. The road is signposted to Combwich, amongst other places. Proceed for a mile, then turn right to Combwich. The pub is on the circular road which winds through the village.

O.S. sheet 182, ref: 258424

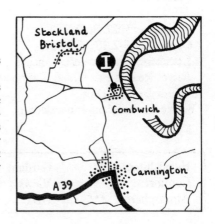

16
LAMB INN
Four Forks, Spaxton, Somerset

Free House

Telephone: (027 867) 350
Open: 11.30-2.30; 6-10.30
Lunchtime and evening snacks
Beers: Real Ales
Wines by the glass
Large garden, but no childrens' facilities

Furnishings:	★	Garden:	★★★★	Cleanliness:	★★
Comfort:	★★	Views:	★★	Toilets:	★
Atmosphere:	★★	OBT:	★★★★	Parking:	★★

Many pubs have gardens, but few of them are so delightful as to demand a visit on a summer day with blue skies. This is the case with the Lamb Inn at Four Forks. Indeed, rather than describe it as a pub with a garden, I prefer to think of it as a garden with a pub.

It is, of course, a personal view. I quite understand that the taste of the beer, or the range of the menu, is more important to some people. But I hope and suspect that some of you will relish the chance to visit a pub simply because it has a garden to delight the senses. Not only that, but the Lamb Inn is about as well removed from the beaten track as you are likely to find, and it may well be that you will enjoy its horticulture undisturbed.

If you are a connoisseur of pub gardens, you will know that even the good ones tend to conform to a stereotype – picnic tables on a more-or-less well cut lawn, paths for conveying food and drink from the pub itself, maybe a childrens' swing or a climbing frame. In the less loved ones, you may spy the occasional potato crisp packet wafting in the breeze. Commercial pressures mean that many pub gardens are regarded as an extension of the sales area, where families with children can be accommodated without flouting the law.

The Lamb's garden is different. It made me feel like a privileged guest. Although larger than a "cottage garden", it has the same sheltered feeling and many of the same flowers – including marvellous roses and dahlias. On a sunsoaked day in late summer I saw more butterflies – Painted Ladies, Peacocks, and Tortoiseshells – in ten minutes than I had seen in the previous three months. And I dared to imagine that, in Four Forks at least, the agricultural chemicals which have so decimated our butterflies in the name of Progress were being used less profligately than elsewhere.

There are just a couple of tables and a few chairs in this lovely place. I hope that my recommendation will not change that, and that you, dear readers, will contrive to spread your visits out so that the garden can stay the way it is. Could you perhaps manage a midweek lunchtime in June or September?

The pub itself is an old, I guess early 19th century, building with lounge and public bars, giving access to the garden via a large archway. There is a reasonable amount of parking and level wheelchair access.

HOW TO GET THERE: The village of Spaxton, and the hamlet of Four Forks, are about 4 miles west of Bridgwater. Take the A39 from Bridgwater towards Minehead. About a mile beyond the village of Cannington, and just past some overhead electricity cables, turn left into a narrow lane signposted to Charlynch. After a mile turn right at a T-junction. After a further half-mile, proceed over the Four Forks crossroads, and you will find the pub on your right.

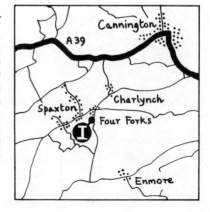

O.S. sheet 182, ref: 233368

17
GEORGE INN
Middlezoy, Somerset

Free House

Telephone: (0823) 69215
Open: 12-2.30; 7-11
Lunchtime and evening meals (not Monday); snacks
Beers* Butcombe Bitter; Cotleigh Tawny Bitter
Wines by the glass
Accommodation

Furnishings:	★★★	Garden:	★	Cleanliness:	★★★
Comfort:	★★	Views:	★★	Toilets:	★★
Atmosphere:	★★★	OBT:	★★	Parking:	★★★

Before the monks of Glastonbury encouraged their tenants to start reclamation of the Somerset Levels in the 12th century, the villages of Middlezoy, Weston Zoyland, and Chedzoy were surrounded, if not by permanent water, at least by marshland crossed by causeways. King's Sedgemoor Drain, gouged out in the 1790's, helped complete the process. So you now need a little imagination, as you approach the island village of Middlezoy perched on a little mound, to recall its former insecurity.

Neither the George Inn nor Middlezoy itself is chic or in any way pretentious. I am confident that the local people, given their historic struggles, would not have it otherwise. The pub is close to the village centre, within shouting distance of two working farms, and close to two thatched cottages decorated with equally thatched birds. There is a wide mix of brick and stone, tile and thatch, in the local buildings, so that the village presents an interesting but somewhat motley appearance. The pub has a small raised terrace at the front with a couple of picnic tables, and some huge slate steps to the doorway. There's parking at the back for about 15 cars, and extra space in the lane. The rear entrance to the pub, via the car park, looks as if it may be reasonable for a wheel chair.

The George Inn has a medium size lounge bar on one side, and a rather larger public bar on the other. I must say I prefer the latter. It has a superb, indeed monumental, slate floor, with a fine old fireplace, beamed ceiling, old settles and a slightly delapidated pool table. It is highly atmospheric. However it is by no means dainty, and if you come in delicate mood you may feel happier in the more modern but rather less interesting lounge – fairly comfortable and looking a bit like a restaurant, with a red carpet, cushioned chairs and benches, and an open fireplace with a stove.

Depending on the weather and perhaps also your mood, Sedgemoor with its criss-crossed rhines and flat unsurfaced droves can seem either a land of light and open skies, or a somewhat forbidding, even melancholy, place. If you feel like indulging the latter mood, I suggest a visit to the site of the Battle of Sedgemoor, tucked away in gentle-looking meadows at the back of Weston Zoyland, where in 1685 the brave but ragged followers of Monmouth's rebellion were routed in the last battle fought on English soil.

HOW TO GET THERE: Middlezoy lies just off the A372 about 6 miles east of Bridgwater. Turn off the main road into the village at the crossroads, keep left after about 100 yards, and you will find the inn a further 150 yards along on the left-hand side.

O.S. sheet 182, ref: 376328

18
MANOR HOUSE INN
Ditcheat, Somerset

Free House

Telephone: (074 986) 276
Open: 12-2.30; 6-10.30
Lunchtime and evening meals and snacks
Beers: Real Ales
Wines by the glass
Garden suitable for children

Furnishings:	★★★	Garden:	★★★	Cleanliness:	★★★
Comfort:	★★★	Views:	★★	Toilets:	★★★
Atmosphere:	★★★★	OBT:	★★	Parking:	★★★

Travelling south towards Ditcheat from Shepton Mallet, the countryside begins to take on the openness and clarity which are so typical of low-lying moorland Somerset. Church towers become more conspicuous, and each village is an event in the landscape. Ditcheat, formerly one of the many estates of Glastonbury Abbey, is a fine example.

I should like to live in Ditcheat. It is a pretty, open, place with a superb Somerset church in a huge and well-kept churchyard, some good solid houses, a couple of shops, a school, and a positive feeling of community. Six members of the Leir family were wise enough to become rectors here from 1699 to 1891, and the family influence has recently been extended in the form of a fine memorial playground.

The buildings of Ditcheat generally reflect its position at the divide between the Somerset hills and moors, with a mixture of stone and brick. However the Manor House Inn is entirely brick – a wonderful old red brick which positively glows a welcome. In truth it has more the air of a private house than a pub, with intimate doorway and pointed windows. There is a good, flat, garden at the back complete with greenhouse and resident rabbit. The car park, also at the back, has rough-surfaced space for about 20 cars, and you will find extra parking in the generous village streets. Wheelchair access to the bar looks reasonably easy via the front door.

The inside of the pub reveals one very long interconnected room – a public bar area at one end with a flagstone floor, leading to a skittle alley; a lounge bar at the other, divided in half by a wall pierced by three pointed arches. The overall feeling is cream and brown with some brass and copper, extremely homely with its local atmosphere. The seating is varied and includes wooden spindle-backs and perhaps ten or a dozen comfortable padded chairs. It really is a delightful spot.

Just a mile or two from Ditcheat, in the village of Wraxall, you can visit one of the vineyards which adorn the south-facing slopes of the Mendips. Not being an expert I must be careful what I say, but it seems that the vines are planted at one fifth the density of continental Europe, on the American and Antipodean pattern, and cultivated high for extra light and ventilation. Whatever the details of the viniculture, I can certainly vouch for the result!

HOW TO GET THERE: Ditcheat is about 2 miles north of Castle Cary. It is signposted from the A37 at Wraxall about 5 miles south of Shepton Mallet, and from the A371 about 2 miles north of Castle Cary. The latter turning is awkward, on a long bend in the main road, and the sign is unclear. The inn is easily found at the centre of Ditcheat, next to the church.

O.S. sheet 183, ref: 626363

19
HALF MOON INN
Horsington, Somerset

Free House

Telephone: (0963) 70140
Open: 11-2.30; 6-11 (also afternoons in summer)
Lunchtime and evening meals and snacks
Beers: Butcombe Bitter; Hook Norton Ale; Wadworth 6X
Wine List; Wines by the glass
Families welcome; Garden suitable for children
Dogs allowed in garden, but not in bars
Accommodation (7 double rooms)

Furnishings:	★★	Garden:	★★★	Cleanliness:	★★★
Comfort:	★★★	Views:	★★	Toilets:	★★
Atmosphere:	★★★	OBT:	★★	Parking:	★★★★

Horsington, at the very edge of Somerset, has the good sense to lie just far enough from the main road to preserve its peace and quiet. It's a charming village with plenty of attractive buildings, seemingly unruffled by the modern rush. Close to its centre you will find the Half Moon Inn, a large and imposing 16th-century stone building with a lovely roof, in a rural setting of trees, meadows, and cottages.

There is a very good garden, split into several parts on several levels, one of them with climbing frames and a slide. This must often prove a delight to families, and I notice that the pub has already decided to extend its opening hours through the afternoon in the summer months. At the back, approached along a slightly tatty side-lane, is a generous park for about 30 cars, with space for 8 or 10 more at the front of the pub. Wheelchair access looks impossible through the front door, but there is a side entrance which should be easier.

Inside you will find a large and pleasant lounge bar, extended back on the right to give a carvery, busy at weekends. There is a separate restaurant. The bar has a huge stone fireplace at each end, a carpeted floor, and wooden furniture including comfortable chairs and window seats. The bar itself is newly constructed in wood, chiming in reasonably well with the uncluttered brown and beige feeling of the room. I know that the Half Moon offers a warm welcome to children, for whom the considerable amount of space – both inside and out – must be a special bonus.

I am sure you will enjoy Horsington, especially if you have time to stroll a hundred yards down the lane and turn off by the duckpond. There's an ancient cross of Ham Hill stone marking the site of the former village market and, eventually, the village church. The churchyard has some fine yew trees and unusually open views across sheep-strewn meadows of the Stour valley to the Dorset hills. The squat church tower, typically east-Somerset and complete with clock, tops a delightful building which – as so often – seems enormous for any likely congregation. Maybe the thought is wayward; but it tends to be confirmed by a notice proclaiming that in 1819 the number of sittings was increased from 300 to 500, of which 280 are reserved " free and unappropriated for ever". It is hard to believe that the population of little Horsington ever justified such generosity!

HOW TO GET THERE: Travel south from Wincanton on the A357. Horsington lies just off the main road to the left, after about 3 miles. There are two or three lanes in quick succession leading into the village. It doesn't much matter which one you take, since the village is small, and the Half Moon is close to its centre.

O.S. sheet 183, ref: 702238

20
CAT HEAD
Chiselborough, Somerset

Gibbs Mew

Telephone: (093 588) 231
Open: 12-2.30; 7-11 (closed Monday lunchtime)
Lunchtime and evening meals and snacks (not Sunday evening)
Beers: Gibbs Mew Wiltshire Bitter; Salisbury Best;
Bishops Tipple
Wines by the glass
Accommodation

Furnishings:	★★★	Garden:	★★	Cleanliness:	★★★
Comfort:	★★	Views:	★★	Toilets:	★★
Atmosphere:	★★★	OBT:	★★	Parking:	★

The outside of the Cat Head at Chiselborough is in the marvellous honey-coloured Ham Hill stone, made even more inviting by Virginia creepers and flowers. Indeed the whole village of Chiselborough seems a flower-filled place, tucked away among the small hills which protrude, noselike, from the southern margins of the Somerset Levels. Next to the pub you will find some lovely cottage gardens, and along a side lane a delightful church with a rebuilt Norman arch, a famous peal of bells, and a memorial to one Agnes Baker revealing – on very close inspection – an unexpected skull.

The main bar of the pub, extended sideways over a former pond to give a double room, has a marvellous flagstone floor. Some of the individual stones must cover fifteen square feet or more, and I gather they rest on brick supports. Of course a stone floor, even when majestic, is never as cosy as polished wood or a carpet, and the bar has a rather basic feeling which makes a surprising contrast with the building's flower-bedecked exterior. Nevertheless I like it for its unfussy, solid, character which shows every bit of its four hundred years. The walls are part-stone, part-rendered and painted cream. There are a few pictures and photos, some silver trophies, and an old upright piano to lighten the atmosphere. The furniture consists of wooden tables, spindle-back chairs, and two fine old settles with generous cushions.

You may like to know that there is an attractive restaurant on the other side of the front door which panders rather more to creature-comforts, and a garden at the back of the pub. Car parking is not very easy, and you will have to make do with nearby village lanes which, fortunately, do not exactly hum with traffic. A wheelchair user will find two steps at the front door, and may prefer the side entrance to the bar.

Chiselborough lies in a lovely, relatively unknown, part of the West Country. To the north, the fascinating flatness of the Somerset Levels with its wide horizons; in Chiselborough itself, and the neighbouring villages of Norton sub Hamdon and West Chinnock, the feeling of having escaped from the strong winds into much more gentle, intimate, countryside; just two or three miles away, one of the National Trust's West Country gems at Montacute; and if you feel like a slightly longer excursion to the south, Dorset, Chesil Bank, and the sea.

HOW TO GET THERE: Chiselborough lies just off the B3165, about 6 miles west of Yeovil. Travelling south on the B3165 from its junction with the A3088, towards Crewkerne, bear left into a lane after about a mile and a half, signposted to Chiselborough. Turn left again after 400 yards at a narrow crossroads, amongst trees. The pub is 200 yards on the right, almost opposite the church.

O.S. sheet 193, ref: 467148

21
ROYAL OAK INN
Luxborough, Somerset

Free House

Telephone: (0984) 40319
Open: 11-2.30 (Sun 12-3); 6-11 (Sun 7-10.30)
Lunchtime and evening meals and snacks
Beers: Flowers IPA; Dorset IPA; Palmers IPA;
      Exmoor Gold; Eldridge Pope Royal Oak
Family room; Garden suitable for children
Dogs admitted

Furnishings:	★★★	Garden:	★	Cleanliness:	★★
Comfort:	★★	Views:	★★	Toilets:	★★
Atmosphere:	★★★★	OBT:	★★★★	Parking:	★★

I have to admit that the name of the pub, and the name of the village, conjured up in me quite the wrong impression. Surely the Royal Oak Inn sounds a bit grand? And how about Luxborough; can it be as substantial as its name implies – like Peterborough, say, or Scarborough? I hoped not.

Travelling the diminutive lanes to Luxborough past sheep-strewn valleys and isolated farms, my fears evaporated. Here, within ten miles of the Megacamps of Minehead, is a hilly tract of England as rural and unspoiled as you are likely to find. I should add that the last two or three of those miles may try your patience sorely, but as you descend from the higher Churchtown end of little Luxborough into its deeper Kingsbridge end, you are likely to feel transported back twenty, fifty, or – for all I know – a hundred years.

The feeling lingers on reaching the Royal Oak, half-hidden in a minute valley bottom where to share the available territory with its four or five neighbours demands a certain flexibility, a certain lack of push. I'm not sure how long the pub has been here, but in any case it has moulded itself into the very fabric of the place, and looks immovable. I just hope that the car park, being dug out of the hillside as I write, will not destroy the feeling of glorious isolation.

Drop down the steps to the front door, and you will see that others, too, have questioned the wisdom of the name. For there (if memory does not fail me) is written "The Blazing Stump". Enter and you will see why. Even in mild mid-October the fire is lit, and there are enough logs piled against the massive fireplace to keep an ordinary blaze alive till mid-December. This is presumably the public bar, as opposed to the lounge bar at the back, and is, in the best possible sense, "unimproved". I plead that it should stay so – plain stone-flagged floor; marvellous beams; simple furniture with friendly, slightly tatty, upholstery; a small restaurant leading off, with a few unpretentious tables, and no concessions whatsoever to modern frills. As if all this were not enough, the long thin lounge bar at the back offers further delights of a basic kind, with exposed timbers, another fire, an old harmonium, and a cat called Polly who is quite likely to steal the softest chair.

This is no place for the fainthearted, but I suspect you will find it hard to drag yourself away.

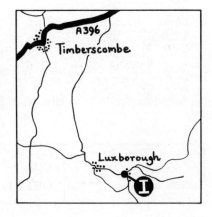

HOW TO GET THERE: Luxborough is best approached via the A396 between Dunster and Wheddon Cross. Travelling out of Dunster, I suggest staying on the A road until you reach Timberscombe, then turning left at its centre up a steep lane between cottages. Continue for two and a half miles, then turn left at a crossroads to Luxborough. Wind through the village past the church, and you will find the inn after another half mile in a valley.

O.S. sheet 181, ref: 984377

22
ROYAL OAK INN
Withypool, Somerset

Free House

Telephone: (064 383) 506
Open: 11-2.30 (Sun 12-2); 6-11 (Sun 7-10.30)
Lunchtime snacks; Evening meals and snacks
Beers: Ruddles County; Ushers best Bitter
Wine List; House Wines; Wines by the glass
Dogs admitted
Accommodation (6 double and 2 single rooms)

Furnishings:	★★★	Garden:	★	Cleanliness:	★★★
Comfort:	★★★	Views:	★★	Toilets:	★★
Atmosphere:	★★★★	OBT:	★★★	Parking:	★★

Rising close to the north Somerset coast at Pinkworthy (or is it Pinkery?) pond, the river Barle decides to do the difficult thing by journeying east and south to Exeter and the English Channel. In the meantime it passes the magical Tarr Steps, and visits the two delightful Exmoor villages of Simonsbath and Withypool. Withypool is the more off the beaten track, and boasts a fine stone bridge, a church, a garage, a village shop, perhaps fifty houses – and the Royal Oak Inn.

The Royal Oak is a small hotel as well as a pub, and I gather that its food has recently been described in the national press as a culinary match for London's West End. It has famous historical associations too, for R.D.Blackmore stayed here whilst writing *Lorna Doone* in 1866. If you approach along the lane from the east, it looks quite a sizeable building, with white tables and chairs under parasols on a front terrace. Here is the main entrance to the hotel, restaurant, and residents' lounge. Approaching from the other direction the Royal Oak looks a lot smaller, since you see mainly the additional Rod Room bar which fronts directly on to the lane. This is the bar you are more likely to use if you drop by for an hour or two for a drink or food.

Withypool is hunting country, and the bar's decorations reflect it with hunting pictures, a stag's head, a fine pair of antlers and several foxy remnants which have seen more active days. If, like me, you prefer man's gentler relationships with the animal world, you will probably warm rather more to the pictures of Katrina and Bonnie which adorn the walls. There is a good brown carpet, ceiling beams interspersed with smoky cream paint, cushioned spindle-back chairs and wall-benches, a fine open fire, and a general feeling of rural well-being. The gents' loo is up a flight of steps, but, apart from that, wheelchair access seems straightforward. Outside there's a car park for about 15 cars, with additional space in the lane.

I have already mentioned Tarr Steps, which you must visit if you can. Unfortunately they are very famous, so I recommend a visit out-of-hours or out-of-season. There is also a fine walk from the steps along the tree-lined Barle valley back towards Withypool. And if you prefer the high places, how about the majestic Dunkery Beacon, some seventeen hundred feet above the sea, with wonderful views over Exmoor and the Bristol Channel?

HOW TO GET THERE: Withypool lies about 10 miles south-west of Minehead. It is easily reached from the B3223 by taking a well signposted turning about 7 miles north of Dulverton. Withypool is about a mile along the lane, after a steep descent, and the inn is at the near end of the village.

O.S. sheet 181, ref: 847356

59

23
GRAMPUS
Lee, Devon

Free House

Telephone: (0271) 62906
Open: 11-2.30; 6-11
Lunchtime and evening meals and snacks
Beers: Flowers Original; Flowers IPA
Wines by the glass
Family room; Garden suitable for children

Furnishings:	★★★	Garden:	★★★	Cleanliness:	★★
Comfort:	★★	Views:	★★	Toilets:	★★
Atmosphere:	★★★	OBT:	★★★	Parking:	★★★

Until recently I had not heard of a grampus. My *Concise Oxford Dictionary* proved enlightening: "a kind of blowing spouting dolphin-like cetacean; a person who breathes loud". Although I approached the Grampus at Lee with some trepidation, there was no need to worry; the inn sign makes clear that the grampus in question is the whale-like variety, but I can assure you that there is no blowing or spouting in the vicinity.

Devon has more than one village of Lee, and at first attempt I chose the wrong one. This Lee is on wild coastline west of Ilfracombe, and has its own small bay – hardly a bucket and spade place, even though the local shops pretend otherwise. I understand that when the tide is out you can reach a sheltered cove with sand, or very fine shingle. There is quite a good car park down by the water, which probably gets very full in high summer – and a cottage decorated with shells.

Surely the best way to arrive in Lee is via the Somerset and North Devon Coast Path, which drops down into the village just inland from the bay. You will then have to strike a few hundred yards further inland to find the Grampus, set amongst cottages in the main part of the village. The pub is on a narrow side lane which rapidly converges into a track, so its entrance is via the car park and garden at the back. There is good parking for about 25 cars. The situation of the pub is level, but there are steps at the entrance to the garden and doorway, which might be difficult for a wheelchair.

In warm weather the Grampus seems an outside sort of place. You can enjoy a sunny garden with lawn and flowers, and seats arranged along the outside wall of the fine old slate-roofed building. At the far end there are about 20 picnic tables, some under a wooden awning, which obviously appeal to families. This part of the garden is a bit tatty with outbuildings, but the children seem to appreciate the rabbit, comfortably housed.

The inside of the pub has a long main bar with wooden chairs and settles. Apart from the lack of cushions, it has a warm and homely feeling, emphasised by a luxurious carpet. I very much like the atmosphere here – pleasantly informal, without being rowdy. There's a darts board, pool table, and games machine in a separate area at the far end. I confidently recommend the Grampus to you, secure in the knowledge that it is gentle and good-natured, without unpleasant vices.

HOW TO GET THERE: The villages of Lincombe and Lee are signposted from the B3231 about 2 miles west of Ilfracombe. Follow the lane down through Lincombe, and you will come to Lee after another half-mile. The Grampus is on the left, in a little side lane.

If you come from Ilfracombe via the North Devon Coast Path, turn left inland when you reach Lee Bay, and the Grampus is about 500 yards up the lane.

O.S. sheet 180, ref: 484464

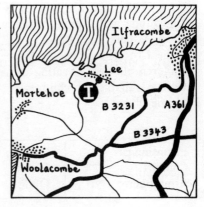

24
OLDE GLOBE
Berrynarbor, Devon

Free House

Telephone: (027 188) 2465
Open: 11-2.30; 6-11 (7-11 in Winter)
Lunchtime and evening meals and snacks
Beers: Ushers Best Bitter
Wine List; House wines; Wines by the glass
Children allowed in eating areas and restaurant
Garden suitable for children
Skittle alley

Furnishings:	★★	Garden:	★★	Cleanliness:	★★★
Comfort:	★★★	Views:	★★	Toilets:	★★★
Atmosphere:	★★★	OBT:	★★	Parking:	★

Berrynarbor is about three miles east of Ilfracombe, tucked a mile back from the dramatic North Devon coast. Approaching via the A399 on a fine day, the sea of Combe Martin Bay looks positively mediterranean. The main ebb and flow of the Bristol Channel, which gives its higher reaches such a muddy reputation, is well to the east. This is a place of stone and cliff, and as you drop down the long valley and through the small town of Combe Martin, you may feel the closeness of The Great Hangman towering a thousand feet above the sea.

True to North Devon form, the lanes to Berrynarbor are narrow and twisty, and when you reach the picture-postcard village you will see that it is hemmed in by steeply wooded hills. There are many white-painted cottages, some lovely gardens, a church, a shop or two, and the Olde Globe. I was told that the pub used to house the masons who built the church in the 13th century. It is a common story about old pubs, and I am unsure whether to believe it; but whatever the details there seems little doubt that the Olde Globe is very olde indeed.

Parking is a problem in Berrynarbor. The pub has a small private car park, but even three or four cars are enough to fill it up. Unless you arrive at the equivalent of a Monday lunchtime in late October, I strongly recommend you try the village car park up the hill from the church, covering the last three hundred yards to the Olde Globe on foot. As you will gather, this is not an easy place for wheelchairs.

Outside the front of the pub there is the small, sloping, car park, and an even smaller terrace. Through a gate you will find quite an attractive side garden with 6 or 7 picnic tables. Inside, there are several small rooms with low-beamed ceilings, arranged around a central serving bar, and a restaurant on the left. Seating is a wide range of chairs, stools, window seats and benches, most with decent cushions. The walls are heavily decorated with pictures and curios, so that the whole place seems full of brass, iron, and leather – perhaps a little topheavy, but full of individuality. Although the rooms are small, the overall amount of space is quite surprising. Towards the back there is a snooker table, and a larger room with a skittle alley.

It seems there is plenty going on at the Olde Globe – including, two days after my last visit, some scheduled entertainment by the Muddiford and Milltown Morris Men.

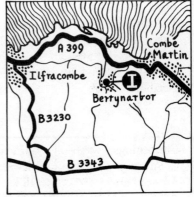

HOW TO GET THERE: Berrynarbor is well signposted from the A399 about 3 miles east of Ilfracombe and 1 mile west of Combe Martin. Lanes to the village are narrow. The pub is about 100 yards down from the church, on a narrow and steep lane. It is a good idea to use the village car park, which is signposted just above the church, and is about 300 yards from the pub.

O.S. sheet 180, ref: 559467

25
EXETER INN
Chittlehamholt, Devon

Free House

Telephone: (07694) 281
Open: 11-2.30; 6-11
Lunchtime and evening meals and snacks
Beers: Ushers Best Bitter; Websters Yorkshire Bitter
Wines by the glass
Children allowed in eating area
Accommodation

Furnishings:	★★★	Garden:	★	Cleanliness:	★★★
Comfort:	★★★	Views:	★★	Toilets:	★★★
Atmosphere:	★★★	OBT:	★★★★	Parking:	★★★

You are unlikely to come across the hamlet of Chittlehamho. 5 miles south-west of South Molton as the crow flies, it is somew.. Devon lanes. If you deliberately seek it out, I have to admit you will no. great deal to attract your attention – apart from two or three fine thatche. cottages, and the delightful Exeter Inn.

The lanes leading to Chittlehamholt require perseverance. At times it seems unlikely that the signposts actually mean what they say, and it comes as quite a surprise to find a substantial and well appointed pub in such a tiny place. The lovely old thatched building, turned sideways onto the lane, has its pub part at one end and accommodation at the other. There is a small paved outside area at the front with two or three picnic tables, and a level car park for about a dozen cars. Wheelchair access seems good.

The inside of the Exeter Inn is thoroughly welcoming. There is a fairly large, comfortable, beamed main bar area with a fine open fireplace. At the back is a long and narrow additional space with tables and benches for customers wishing to eat. Seating is a mixture of wooden chairs, stools, and benches, most of them cushioned. Some old beer barrels have been cleverly and attractively modified, and pressed into service as extra chairs. To judge by the lengthy menu, advertised on slates hung on the walls, you need not leave feeling hungry.

I tend to be rather sceptical of gimcracks in a pub, because they can so easily spoil its looks. In this case, however, I really enjoyed the huge collection of matchboxes arranged around the old beams. They brought back memories of childhood, when there were so many more varieties around. I know that matchbox collecting can be a serious pursuit, and imagine this could be something of a Mecca if you are involved. There is also a good selection of banknotes from many different times and countries. If you are visiting the Exeter Inn from some far-off place, maybe you should present them with a trophy.

As I have hinted, Chittlehamholt the village is a rather modest spot. If you have an hour to spare, how about Chittlehampton? It lies 3 miles to the north, just the other side of the B3227, and has a lovely square complete with gaudy village pump and a huge and interesting church.

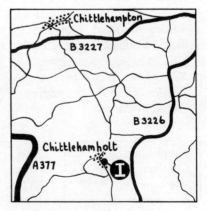

HOW TO GET THERE: The village is signposted from the B3227 between South Molton and Umberleigh, about 2 miles from Umberleigh. The lane is straightforward but narrow, and you will reach Chittlehamholt after about two and a half miles. Proceed through the village and the inn is on your left-hand side.

Chittlehamholt is also signposted from the B3226 south-west of South Molton, and from the A377.

O.S. sheet 180, ref: 650208

RLEIGH INN
gh, Devon

Free House

Telephone: (08845) 407
Open: 11-2.30; 6-11 (Fri 5-11)
Lunchtime and evening snacks
Lunchtime meals (not Sunday); Evening meals (not Tuesday)
Beers: Cotleigh Old Buzzard; Cotleigh Tawny Bitter;
        Cotleigh Kingfisher Ale
Wine List; Wines by the glass
Garden suitable for children
Accommodation

Furnishings:	★★★★	Garden:	★★	Cleanliness:	★★★
Comfort:	★★★	Views:	★★	Toilets:	★★
Atmosphere:	★★★★	OBT:	★★★★	Parking:	★★

Please don't go to Butterleigh expecting new-thatched cottages or prize-winning floral displays. It is not the sort of place where film stars flit, or wealthy industrialists spend long weekends. Butterleigh is a very small and quite simple farming village somewhere between Cullompton and Tiverton in East Devon, with none of the trappings of tourist country – and probably none of the problems, either.

If Butterleigh can be described as "unimproved", then so too, in the nicest possible sense, can the Butterleigh Inn. It is charmingly unpretentious. As you drop down the steep lane to make acquaintance for the first time, it is a little hard to square the straightforward Victorian appearance with its sixteenth century origins. Certainly the outside looks nothing special. The building is turned sideways on the lane, with a roughly surfaced car park for about 20 cars at its back, and a cosily sheltered terrace at its front which catches the afternoon and evening sun. Between the two is a footpath leading past a small lawn with a wooden summerhouse for children (and adults, too?). This must be an attractive place in midsummer.

Nevertheless, the main delights of the Butterleigh Inn are to be found inside, with its three rooms each furnished in distinctive style. On the left through a doorway, we have a marvellous smallish lounge bar-cum-restaurant, with a superb open fire, some good wooden furniture, a rich red carpet, and well-chosen brass and copper. A friendly, civilised, place with a warm glow about it. Then in the middle there is a roughish, atmospheric, bar with its own open fire, a darts board, an old pine settle which doubles as a local advertising agency, and some simple wooden furniture casually adorned with the odd cushion or two.

The third room – only fairly recently opened up to public inspection, I believe – is entered via a curtained doorway on the right. It's a lovely little extra space for eating or drinking, with a creamy brown feel about it: a good brown carpet, light walls with some very attractive pictures, and pine wall benches upholstered in a print which tunes in thoughtfully with the rest of the room.

There are not many inns which achieve such happy contrasts of mood and colour, antiquity and comfort. The Butterleigh Inn knows what it wants, and I very much hope it stays that way.

HOW TO GET THERE: Half way along Cullompton's main street, take the narrow, unsignposted turning alongside the Midland Bank. The road soon becomes wider. After about a mile and a half, just over the brow of a hill, turn left at a small crossroads to Butterleigh. After a further mile and a half, turn sharp left at another crossroads, also signposted. Descend into the village and you will find the inn on your right.

O.S. sheet 192, ref: 974083

27
FIVE BELLS
Clyst Hydon, Devon

Free House

Telephone: (08847) 288
Open: 11.30-2.30; 6.30-11
Lunchtime and evening meals and snacks
Beers: Draught Bass; Badger Best Bitter
Wine List; Wines by the glass
Garden suitable for children

Furnishings:	★★	Garden:	★★★	Cleanliness:	★★★
Comfort:	★★★	Views:	★★	Toilets:	★★
Atmosphere:	★★★★	OBT:	★	Parking:	★★★

Since 1890 the name of this delightful pub should really have been Six Bells; for that was when the extra treble was installed in Clyst Hydon's belfry. Going back a lot further, we are told that the village's need for liquid refreshment used to be met by an Alehouse called the Refuge Inn, situated half way along the footpath to the church. But it proved too noisy, and was demoted – or maybe promoted? – to Refuge Cottage. I suspect that the Five Bells, which shows every sign of having started life as a Devon farmhouse, took over at this time. In any case it is situated quite a long way from the church, on the outskirts of the village. It looks very much like another example of the British talent for compromise.

The Five Bells is a fine thatched building, long and low. It is set sideways on a narrow lane in open country, surrounded by the gently rolling farmland of East Devon. There's a good level car park just beyond – a hard surface for about 25 cars, and a rougher one for a further 15 – and a substantial meadow garden with a children's climbing frame and some picnic tables, approached up a few steps. This is in addition to the smaller, cottagey, garden immediately in front of the pub. Wheelchair access would be difficult directly from the car park, or into the main garden, because of steps; but there's also a path from the road to the front door, which looks negotiable.

The spaciousness of the inside comes as rather a surprise. The complete ground floor has been made into a large open-plan bar and restaurant, swallowing up the building's former individual rooms. On the right is an attractive area with dark wooden tables and chairs and a red carpet; in the middle, by the door, a former snug with low ceiling (ladies used to be admitted on Sunday evenings!); and on the left, a comfortable lounge bar area, leading via a short stairway to a substantial restaurant, which bends round the corner and has a lovely open fire. Apart from the snug area, the ceilings are fairly high and beamed. I suppose that, if the restaurant is included, it must be possible to seat seventy or eighty people here without an undue crush. And the overall atmosphere is sufficiently friendly and welcoming that I guess such spacious-ness must often be justified.

HOW TO GET THERE: Clyst Hydon is about 8 miles north-east of Exeter, on the B3176 between Cullompton and Ottery St. Mary. The inn is along a small lane which leaves the B road at the western outskirts of the village. If you come from Cullompton the turning is on an awkward bend which needs care. Proceed along the lane and you will find the inn after about 300 yards.

O.S. sheet 192, ref: 028014

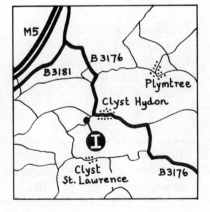

28
BULLERS ARMS
Chagford, Devon

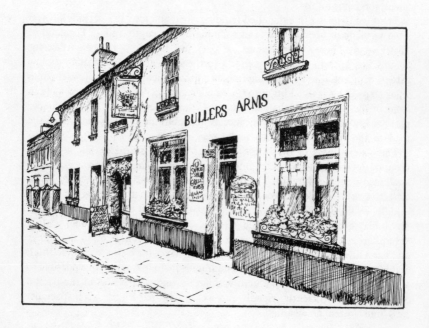

Free House

Telephone: (06473) 2348
Open: 11.30-2.30; 6-11
Lunchtime and evening meals and snacks
Beers: Ushers Best Bitter; Marston Pedigree
Wine List; Wines by the glass; Draught cider

Furnishings:	★★★	Garden:	★	Cleanliness:	★★★
Comfort:	★★★	Views:	★	Toilets:	★★
Atmosphere:	★★★★	OBT:	★	Parking:	★

It is hard not to envy the people of Chagford. It has some lovely buildings, which are kept in very good order, and is situated in fine countryside on the north-eastern edge of Dartmoor. There is a nice balance between boredom and bustle, and the inhabitants, as far as one can judge, are thoroughly contented. On my last visit Chagford seemed a place with a lot of sunshine and very few clouds. It is almost large enough to be called a town, and I suppose it's hardly fair to describe it as off the beaten track. However no major roads pass this way, and you must travel the Devon lanes.

In the midst of this delightfulness stands the Bullers Arms. You will find it in a rather narrow street just off the central square, competing for space with houses and shops. I should straight away mention that the pub has no private parking, and that Chagford has a parking problem. So try to plan your visit for an off-peak time.

The inside of the Bullers Arms is notable mainly for its friendly atmosphere. When I was there at lunchtime it was full of local people, eating as well as drinking, and I have no doubt that they know a good thing when they see it. Unlike many of the Devon pubs described in this book, the feeling is not of antiquity. The ceilings are relatively high and unbeamed, and although the furnishings are rather a mix of styles, the overall effect is pleasantly late-Victorian, or perhaps Edwardian. There is quite a large main bar, apparently formed from three original rooms, and a smaller restaurant towards the back of the building along a passageway. Seating is mixed and fairly comfortable. I noticed a jukebox, but it was not in use, the only noise being the animated chatter of a fair cross-section of Chagford society enjoying itself.

There is a small paved outside area at the back of the pub with 20 or so white plastic chairs and tables, somewhat optimistically described as a beer garden. On my visit there were no signs of plants or trees, but it looked as if plans were afoot to make it greener. A partly constructed wooden awning suggested the future possibility of shelter, and maybe an attractive vine. We shall have to wait and see.

Of all the lovely places to visit near Chagford, may I suggest Castle Drogo, built between 1910 and 1930 by the remarkable Lutyens, and now in the care of the National Trust? It is just 3 miles away, on the far side of the A382.

HOW TO GET THERE: Chagford is best reached by turning off the A382 about 2 miles north of Moretonhampstead. Park where you can when you arrive, and then locate the main square. The Bullers Arms is about 50 yards from the square, along Mill Street.

O.S. sheet 191, ref: 700877

RING OF BELLS

North Bovey, Devon

Free House

Telephone: (0647) 40375
Open: 11-11 (but closed 3-5 in Winter)
Lunchtime and evening meals and snacks
Beers: Wadworth 6X; Halls Plympton Best
Wine List; Wines by the glass
Garden suitable for children
Accommodation

Furnishings:	★★★	Garden:	★★	Cleanliness:	★★
Comfort:	★★★	Views:	★★	Toilets:	★★
Atmosphere:	★★★★	OBT:	★★★	Parking:	★

Even by Devon standards, the lanes leading to North Bovey are high-sided and narrow. In late spring and summer when the hedgerows are in lusty growth, they seem reluctant to let a car pass. If you meet an opposing vehicle, you may need both patience and diplomacy to extricate yourself.

The village is a hilly, intimate, place with many thatched cottages sheltering under the north-eastern slopes of Dartmoor. The river Bovey, rising on the high moor, passes through the village on its way to join the Teign near Newton Abbot, and finally the sea at Teignmouth. Pony trekking and fishing are particularly attractive in these parts.

The Ring of Bells is one of those picture-postcard pubs: ancient, thatched, with huge stone walls and low beams. Fortunately, unlike many other picture-postcard pubs, it is the genuine article, and has not been prettied up for the tourist trade. Outside at the front there is a small garden, and a paved area with a number of picnic tables. Wheelchair access is level, and reasonable into the pub itself if you can manage one or two low ridges. There is no private car park, but the surroundings of the village green offer a fair number of parking spaces. Nevertheless this may be a problem at busy times.

The inside of the pub is a delight. There is a medium size bar on the left, plus two or three small rooms with simple furnishings and fairly comfy wooden seating with cushions. The walls are painted unfussily in beige, setting off the dark beams, and there is at least one fine open fireplace. In one of the rooms you will find a grandfather clock in symbiosis with a wall. The ceilings are generally low, and especially in the restaurant to the right of the front door. It is just as well that we sit down to eat, for the ceiling height here cannot be much above five feet six. It would probably be easier to enter the gents' loo lying down than on one's feet.

An unusual feature of North Bovey is its village green, which has been planted with oak trees, many of them commemorating important occasions over the last hundred years. If you have children with you (or even if you haven't), here is a nice puzzle which can be solved within 100 yards of the pub: On what royal occasions were trees planted; and why was 10th January 1920 a day for high hopes, subsequently dashed?

HOW TO GET THERE: From the crossroads at the centre of Moretonhampstead, take the B3212 towards Princetown. Almost immediately turn left into a narrow lane alongside a newsagent's shop, marked (not very clearly) to North Bovey. You will come to the village after about 2 twisty miles. The pub is at its centre, just off the village green.

O.S. sheet 191, ref: 741838

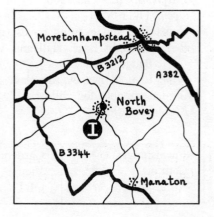

30

MASONS ARMS

Branscombe, Devon

Free House

Telephone: (029 780) 300
Open: 11-11
Lunchtime and evening meals (not Sunday lunch); Snacks
Beers: Draught Bass; Hall and Woodhouse Tanglefoot;
     Badger Best Bitter
Wine List; Wines by the glass
Garden suitable for children
Accommodation

Furnishings:	****	Garden:	***	Cleanliness:	***
Comfort:	***	Views:	***	Toilets:	**
Atmosphere:	***	OBT:	**	Parking:	***

Winding down four hundred feet from South Devon's hinterland towards the coast, one sees the village of Branscombe spreadeagled below. It is the type of village I so love to find – an unspoiled tangle of delightful stone buildings, many of them thatched, huddling in a steep valley bottom almost within sound of the sea.

The Masons Arms, set right in the centre of the village, is quite an establishment. Its front terrace, on two or three levels and extending round one side of the building, comes complete with thatched umbrellas and perhaps thirty wooden tables. The car park is a little rough and sloping (it could hardly be otherwise in Branscombe!), but must be adequate for nearly forty cars. The garden area is well designed and contained by some good walling, giving a feeling of solid character. Although the rear entrance to the pub from the car park involves steps, there is level access to the front door from the road.

The inside is excellent. There's a substantial restaurant on the right of the entrance, and a superb bar on the left, more or less divided in two along its length by a wall with an inbuilt open fireplace. Some of the windows are let deep into massive walls. The paintwork is white, with dark beams and woodwork set off by a restrained use of old brass and copper. The floor, on two or three different levels, is partly slate, partly carpeted. There is a lot of good quality wooden furniture and some cushioned benches. The net result is thoroughly to my taste, and the atmosphere is civilised. I suppose that such a well-known pub must get very busy in the holiday season, but on a brilliant day in early November the patronage was local, and all was calmness and consideration.

When you have enjoyed yourselves in Branscombe, you really must take the lane down to the sea at Branscombe Mouth. It's an easy enough walk, but if you want to go by car you will find a fairly generous car park almost on the beach. The National Trust is fortunately very much in evidence, and the shingle beach and foreshore are cleanly uncluttered. Four-hundred foot cliffs rise up to either side, clad in subtle shades of red and beige and slate. And if you have the energy I suggest a walk up the steep grass slopes of East Cliff, leading on to the dramatic pinnacles of the Hooken Cliff landslip (*circa* 1790), and a 30-mile vista towards Portland Bill.

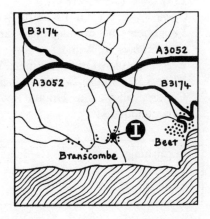

HOW TO GET THERE: Branscombe lies about half a mile back from the coast, roughly midway between Sidmouth and Seaton. It is signposted from several places on the A3052, and although the lanes are generally steep and twisty, you should have little difficulty finding the village. The Masons Arms is towards its eastern end.

O.S. sheet 192, ref: 203888

31
SHIP INN
Axmouth, Devon

Devenish

Telephone: (0297) 21838
Open: 11-2.30 (Sun 12-2.30); 6-11 (Sun 7-10.30)
Lunchtime and evening meals and snacks
(not Fridays in Winter)
Beers★ Cornish Original Bitter; Wessex Royal
Wine List; House Wines; Wines by the glass
Children allowed in Dining Room; Garden also suitable
Dogs admitted

Furnishings:	★★★	Garden:	★★★	Cleanliness:	★★★★
Comfort:	★★★	Views:	★★	Toilets:	★★★
Atmosphere:	★★★	OBT:	★	Parking:	★★

There are not many places where one can watch tawny owls from the comfort of an attractive lounge bar. At least this was my good fortune when I visited the Ship Inn at Axmouth. For the garden at the back of the pub has been partly made over to birds in distress, and the inmates of its substantial aviary are visible from the pub's windows. How the good lady finds time to look after injured and orphaned birds – which, at various times, have included buzzards and kestrels – as well as work in a busy and delightful pub, I cannot imagine. But she is apparently well known as a local samaritan, and is licensed to keep them.

The lounge bar of the Ship is L-shaped, and fairly small. It is rather unusually decorated in light green and mid-green paintwork, with pine tables and chairs, and cushioned window seats covered with an attractive beige-and-green print. The whole effect is light and airy and natural. Amongst the decorations and furnishings are five or six glass-fronted wall cases, specially made to house a marvellous collection of small dolls. I'm no expert in such matters, but it is clear that they must have come from many different countries at many different times, and that they have received loving care over the years.

The outside of the pub is also very attractive. The building faces directly on to the main street of Axmouth, which is, I suppose, too big to be a village, and too small to be a town. All this means that the Ship is not truly off the beaten track, but it is a calm enough spot out of the main summer season. The stone frontage of the building is enlivened by a miniature thatched roof over the main door, somewhat reminiscent of a half-doughnut. There's a well-surfaced flat car park at one side, sufficient for about a dozen cars, with additional parking nearby. Wheelchair entry seems straightforward and level through the front door, or via a side passageway to the lounge bar. Do not be put off by the large white fluffy dogs, which, whatever their temper towards strangers when the pub is closed, seem delightfully relaxed when it is open.

On the far side of the car park – and quite separate from the aviary at the back of the pub – there's a pretty small garden with a few picnic tables and an old apple tree. Although it faces the road, it somehow manages to give the feeling of being pleasantly withdrawn. From here you can sit and watch the rest of Axmouth bustle by.

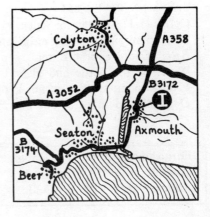

HOW TO GET THERE: Axmouth lies about 5 miles south of Axminster and is served by the B3172 which also goes to Seaton. The pub is easily found on the B road near the centre of Axmouth.

O.S. sheet 192, ref: 258911

32
TAVISTOCK INN
Poundsgate, Devon

Courage

Telephone: (03643) 251
Open: 11-11 (Easter to Sept); 11-3, 6-11 (Winter)
Lunchtime and evening meals and snacks
Beers★ Courage Best Bitter
Wines by the bottle and glass
Family room; Garden is not a play area
Dogs allowed in bars, but not in garden

Furnishings:	★★★★	Garden:	★★★★	Cleanliness:	★★★
Comfort:	★★★	Views:	★★★	Toilets:	★★
Atmosphere:	★★★★	OBT:	★	Parking:	★★★

The Tavistock Inn lies on the B road which snakes from Ashburton up onto Dartmoor. You may therefore question whether it is genuinely off the beaten track. I can only reply that there is not a great deal of traffic outside the obvious holiday periods, and that the pub's other features, including a fine old stone building and a lovely garden, more than compensate.

Poundsgate has a Post Office Stores, a few houses, the pub, and that is about all. The road winds through it so tortuously that traffic is forced to proceed at snail's pace. If you approach from Ashburton you will pass over two wonderful stone bridges, so narrow that they demand one-way traffic and more or less repel holiday coaches. The village itself is on the very edge of Dartmoor, two or three miles below Dartmeet where – not surprisingly – the East and West Dart rivers reinforce each other for their journey to the sea.

When you reach the pub, you will see immediately that it is a building of enormous character. The roof, originally thatched, is now of slate. There is a lovingly-tended garden at the back with picnic tables, and more outside furniture at the front on a hard forecourt. The floral display is so spectacular that it is easy to see why the pub has received prizes for its garden. On the other side of the road is a good car park for about 20 cars. However wheelchair access is hampered by steps to the front door and the garden slope.

The inside of the pub is marvellous. Please do not expect a delicate atmosphere: you might feel out of place in high-heeled shoes or evening dress. But if the idea of an ancient Dartmoor building with stone walls and a superb fireplace appeals, then it is the place for you. The left-hand upright stone of the fireplace looks as if it weighs at least a ton. I also love the high-ceilinged extension bar at the right-hand end of the building, with its fine settles and a majestic wall – a little cavernous, and somehow redolent of highwaymen. Much of the seating is reasonably comfortable, with cushions on both chairs and window seats. The loos are rustic, a little antiquated, and round the back, but they are reasonable.

I long to return to the Tavistock Inn in bleak midwinter when the fires are lit, and the wind blows cruel across the moor.

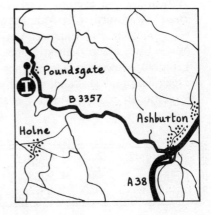

HOW TO GET THERE: The village of Poundsgate is on the B3357 between Ashburton and Princetown, about 5 miles from Ashburton. You can hardly miss the pub, which is at the Dartmoor end of the village.

O.S. sheet 191, ref: 704722

33
WILD GOOSE
Combeinteignhead, Devon

Free House

Telephone: (0626) 872241
Open: 11-2.30 (Sun 12-2.30); 6.30-11 (Sun 7-10.30)
Lunchtime and evening meals and snacks
Beers★ Wadworth 6X; Mill Brewery Janners Ale;
      Golden Hill Exmoor Ale; Marston Pedigree
Wine List; House wines; Wines by the glass
Children allowed in garden (not a "play area")
Dogs admitted at Landlord's discretion
Traditional Jazz on Monday evenings

Furnishings:	★★★★	Garden:	★★	Cleanliness:	★★★
Comfort:	★★★	Views:	★★	Toilets:	★★
Atmosphere:	★★★★	OBT:	★★★	Parking:	★★

As wild geese fly the small village of Combeinteignhead is just 2 miles from Newton Abbot, the same from Shaldon, and about 3 miles from the outskirts of Torquay. A haven of peace within this busy triangle, the village sports a church, a post office, and a diminutive public garden bearing the delightful notice *Queen's Jubilee Garden – Come in and Sit Down.*

Combeinteignhead is attractive without being in any way slick. I was a little disappointed to find that there are no views of the Teign estuary, which is only a few hundred yards away. But if you want these – and some sea air – before sampling the delights of the Wild Goose, you can get down to the water at Coombe Cellars, a few hundred yards to the east of the village.

The Wild Goose is near the church, up the lane towards Stokeinteignhead. It is a narrow place, hemmed in by the surrounding hillside, and the car park, roughly surfaced but big enough for about 30 cars, is a further 75 yards up the lane. Wheelchair access is not particularly easy, and is further complicated by steps at the front door.

The main delights of the pub are reserved for the inside. It is a lovely mid-17th century building, with beamed ceilings and some very attractive furniture. It is easy to believe that the licensee formerly ran an antiques business in Bristol. The main bar is homely but surprisingly large, and there is a good size restaurant at the back. Seating is a wide range of chairs and stools, many comfortably upholstered. There seems to be an efficient and imaginative kitchen, and I have little doubt that the food is good. Behind the pub is a small garden with a few picnic tables.

Among the many attractive furnishings is a mid-Victorian engraving depicting *Charles The First Parting With His Children.* This tragedy of 1649 must have been close to the date when the pub was built. If you look a little closer, you will see that the Victorian tapestry on the opposite wall is a copy of the engraving. Apparently the present owners, having had the tapestry for some years, came across the engraving and decided they should keep each other company. And it is a comment on the delightfulness of the Wild Goose that, providing you arrive early enough, you have a good chance of studying them from the comfort of a chaise longue!

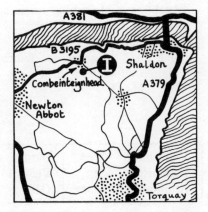

HOW TO GET THERE: Combeinteign-head is readily approached from Shaldon or Newton Abbot via the B3195. However the road is narrow and twisty (and busy in summer). There is a triple junction at the centre of the village. Take the lane towards Stokeinteignhead, and you will find the pub about 100 yards up on the right. The car park is a further 75 yards, also on the right.

O.S. sheet 202, ref: 903715

34
CHURCH HOUSE INN
Rattery, Devon

Free House

Telephone: (0364) 42220
Open: 11-2.30 (Sun 12-2.30); 6-11 (Sun 7-10.30)
Lunchtime and evening meals and snacks
Beers★ Courage Best Bitter; Courage Directors
      Guest beers
Wine List; House wines; Wines by the glass
Children allowed in small patio garden
Dogs allowed

Furnishings:	★★★★	Garden:	★★	Cleanliness:	★★★
Comfort:	★★★	Views:	★★	Toilets:	★
Atmosphere:	★★★★	OBT:	★★★	Parking:	★★

Winding through the lanes to Rattery, you will see its quaint, squat, church spire from some way off. Not surprisingly Church House Inn is next door, and the two have a long and close connection. The date proudly proclaimed on its front wall – 1028 – may only apply to a small part of the present fabric, but even so there seems little doubt that this is one of the oldest pub buildings in England. I was told that it originally housed the masons who made the church, although this is a little difficult to square with dates given in the church leaflet. Never mind, the story is a good one, and who am I to quibble over the odd century among so many?

There's a small, sunny, front patio with a few picnic tables encircled by a hedge. The car park is shared with the church and also, I think, the village, and offers level parking for about 25 cars. The general surroundings are rural and open, with both pub and church set in the upper part of the village.

The special character of the Church House Inn is obvious as soon as you enter the front door. There is a superb, long, low-beamed bar stretching much of the length of the building. It boasts a wealth of old oak, and just the right amount of gleaming brass and copper. The seating is full of charm - spindle-back chairs and armchairs with comfortable cushions, window seats, and two marvellous old chairs with carved backs which could well have churchy origins. Between the main bar and a dining area on its right is a fine oak screen with upright timbers and a massive crosspiece. All in all this is a lovely place with bags of atmosphere, and there is ample evidence of interesting food, including local and vegetarian specialities.

Since I have lavished so much praise on the pub, I think it only fair to mention the loos, which dwell in outbuildings. Suffice it to say that the gents', at least, is less enchanting than the rest of the facilities (I am not however for one moment suggesting that it dates from 1028!).

St. Mary's church, whose lych-gate can almost be touched from the pub garden, has a delightful Norman interior and is well worth a few quiet moments of your time. And while on the subject of visits, how about the attractions of nearby Buckfastleigh – its Benedictine monastery, steam railway, and butterfly farm?

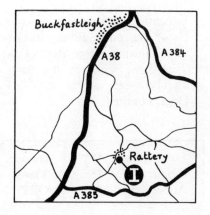

HOW TO GET THERE: The small village of Rattery is well signposted from the A38 about 2 miles south of Buckfastleigh, and also from the A385 about 4 miles west of Totnes. Be prepared for narrow lanes as soon as you leave the main road. The pub is easily found, being next to the church on high ground at the southern end of the village.

O.S. sheet 202, ref: 740616

83

35

PETER TAVY INN

Peter Tavy, Devon

Free House

Telephone: (082 281) 348
Open: 11.30-2.30 (Sun 12-3); 6.30-11 (Sun 7-10.30)
Lunchtime and evening meals and snacks
Beers★ Butcombe Bitter; Blackawton 44; Wadworth 6X;
      Eldridge Pope Royal Oak; Courage Directors
Wine List; Wines by the glass
Family room; Garden suitable for children
Dogs admitted

Furnishings:	★★★	Garden:	★★	Cleanliness:	★★★
Comfort:	★★	Views:	★★	Toilets:	★
Atmosphere:	★★★★	OBT:	★★★	Parking:	★★

The river Tavy, which gives its name to the villages of Peter Tavy and Mary Tavy and the town of Tavistock, is born on wildest Dartmoor, alongside the river Dart. But the two part company in infancy, the Dart breaking eastwards towards the sea at Dartmouth, the Tavy striking west and south to Plymouth. Peter Tavy, a small and unprepossessing village just three miles from Tavistock, is at the western edge of the moor, brooded over by White Tor and Cox Tor from a thousand feet above.

You will find the Peter Tavy Inn along a short side-lane, adjacent to the church. At first it is a little hard to believe the lane leads anywhere much, but then quite suddenly the inn comes into view. It is surprisingly substantial for such a spot - a fine 15th century stone building with a small paved area at the front, and a small but rather charming walled garden.

The inside of the pub is genuine, homely, and unpretentious. The main room has a very low, quaint, bar area, and I imagine that an advertisement for staff would have to specify a maximum height of about five feet four. A church-like window is let into one of the massive walls. There are lovely old beams and woodwork, and a variety of wooden seating – unfortunately, without cushions. On the right-hand side, and taking up quite a large amount of the building, is an excellent kitchen. I always like it when cooks and their equipment are visible; it gives the feeling that there is nothing to be ashamed of, and bolsters confidence. In the case of the Peter Tavy Inn, it seems that guests are actively encouraged to enter the hallowed ground and choose their own dishes, which include an unusually good vegetarian selection.

Outside there is parking for about 10 cars, with level access for a wheelchair. If you arrive in a car at a busy time, it would probably be sensible to park elsewhere in the village. I should perhaps mention that the loos, which are tucked away at a corner of the building, are of the rustic variety.

You can quite easily get up onto Dartmoor from the southern end of the village, and if you have not yet taken the B3357 to Princetown, I strongly recommend you do so. Barring mist or low cloud the scenery is superb, with high tors very much in evidence and Dartmoor ponies roaming wild.

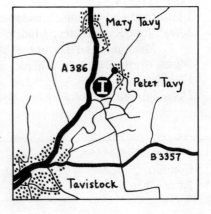

HOW TO GET THERE: Peter Tavy is easily reached from the A386 about 2 miles north of Tavistock. Once you leave the main road, keep bearing left to reach the village. The inn is along a side-lane next to the church.

You can also reach Peter Tavy by turning off the B3357 about 2 miles east of Tavistock. However the route is difficult unless you are good with maps.

O.S. sheet 191, ref: 512778

36
MOUNTAIN INN
Lutton, Devon

Free House

Telephone: (0752) 837247
Open: 11-3; 6-11
Lunchtime and evening snacks, evening meals
Beers★ Butcombe Bitter; Golden Hill Exmoor Ale;
        Mountain and Dartmoor Strong; Murphy's Stout
Wines by the bottle and glass
Family room
Dogs allowed on terrace, but not in bars

Furnishings:	★★★★	Garden:	★★	Cleanliness:	★★★★
Comfort:	★★★	Views:	★★★	Toilets:	★★★
Atmosphere:	★★★★	OBT:	★★★★	Parking:	★

The Mountain Inn at Lutton is a delightful pub in a fine setting. An old stone building wedged into a line of terraced cottages, it surveys the rolling hills of South Devon from a high vantage point on the fringe of Dartmoor. You may have a little difficulty finding it, but I promise you the effort will be amply rewarded. I should however add that the Mountain Inn is known far beyond the hamlet of Lutton. So try to visit it at an uncrowded time, avoiding the main holiday season.

The pub is approached up a steep lane, so narrow that it seems unlikely to lead anywhere except trouble. Then suddenly, perched against the hillside, you will see the object of your journey, quaint and enticing. If you arrive at a busy time you may have difficulty parking, because there is space for only six or seven cars. So the wise motorist will probably leave the car on the main road (if that is the right word for it!), and do the last two hundred yards on foot. I should perhaps add that this is hardly a place for wheelchairs; even if you reach the pub, there are steep ramps to negotiate.

The outside of the building has recently been rerendered, and modestly extended, but not enough to spoil its intimacy. There is a small paved area at the front where, with luck, you can join the cats in the sunshine. If you claim one of the two or three picnic tables on the small raised terrace, you will have marvellous views to the west. A large and healthy-looking vine extends over the front door, suggesting that England is hardly the damp foggy place of folklore, and promising a good supply of black grapes in October.

The inside of the pub fully lives up to expectations. The overall feeling is of ancient stone and wood, with three small rooms charmingly furnished. There is a large open fireplace, and I can imagine the joy of a cold November evening in its company. Overall, space is somewhat at a premium, but there is just enough of it to contain an old harmonium and some good antique furniture. The loos are as welcoming as expected, and more tasteful than one would dare to hope. Although I did not sample the food myself, a local assured me of its excellence.

It is hard to fault the Moutain Inn. As you will by now appreciate, I am one of its many admirers.

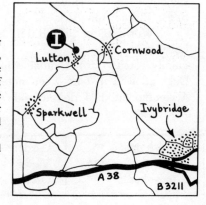

HOW TO GET THERE: Lutton is near the rather larger village of Cornwood, which is signposted from the Ivybridge junction of the A38. Go to the centre of Cornwood, and turn off to Lutton by the side of the Cornwood Inn. As you enter Lutton, the Mountain Inn is signposted up a narrow lane on your right hand side. It may be best to park at the bottom, and walk the last two hundred yards.

O.S. sheet 202, ref: 596595

37

MILDMAY COLOURS INN

Holbeton, Devon

Free House

Telephone: (075 530) 248
Open: 11-3 (Sun 12-3); 6-11 (Sun 7-11)
Lunchtime and evening meals and snacks; Carvery upstairs
Beers: Blackawton Ales; Flowers Original;
     Worthington Best Bitter; Stella Artois
Local cider
Family room; Garden suitable for children
Dogs allowed in bars when not busy, and in garden
Accommodation (1 double and 7 twin rooms; Singles in Winter)

Furnishings:	★★	Garden:	★★	Cleanliness:	★★
Comfort:	★★★	Views:	★★	Toilets:	★★
Atmosphere:	★★★	OBT:	★★	Parking:	★★★

If you are on the South Devon coast in the holiday season, you may find the roads and beaches rather full and the towns a little overcrowded. In such circumstances a tactical retreat to a village a few miles back from the coast may help restore equilibrium. I would like to suggest Holbeton, which is well off the main tourist routes. A medium size village in hilly countryside, with a huge and interesting church, it also has an attractive inn called the Mildmay Colours.

Let me first of all enlighten you about the name, which is surely one of the most unusual in Devon. No, it has nothing to do with military flags, or painting in oils, or the riot of herbaceous colour at the front of the building; the colours in this case are racing ones, and the inn takes its name from a certain Lord Mildmay, who was very keen on riding. I confess I am not a horsy person, and I did not discover all the details, but I gather his life ended tragically. No doubt you can find out more if you visit the place yourself, and engage the locals in conversation.

The Mildmay Colours feels, and probably is, mid-to-late Victorian, without the thatched roof or low ceilings of many old Devon inns. It is a pleasing, solid, unpretentious, building in the centre of Holbeton, right next to the church. There is quite a large lounge bar, plus a public bar and a carvery, substantially renovated and redecorated in a mixture of styles. The lounge-bar seating is reasonably comfortable, and includes a number of benches with good cushions. Many of the pictures on the walls, and the wording of its extensive menu, reflect the pub's equestrian interest.

Outside at the back there's a roughly-surfaced car park, sufficient for about 25 cars. It is surrounded by old farm buildings, giving a good rural feeling. If you enter the pub via the back garden, you will see a few picnic tables on a small lawn, and some exotic parrots in a cage. Unfortunately this is not an easy place for wheelchairs, because of slopes and steps.

Before you leave Holbeton, and assuming you have at least some interest in history or architecture, you really must look at the 15th century church, with its wonderful woodwork and elaborate pulpit – "a treasure-house of splendid carving guarded by rich doors".

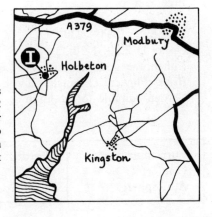

HOW TO GET THERE: Holbeton is well signposted from the A379 about 2 miles west of Modbury. Shortly after leaving the main road, you will need to bear left to the village, reached after a further mile. The inn is at its centre, next to the church.

O.S. sheet 202, ref: 613501

38
FIRST AND LAST
Ermington, Devon

Free House

Telephone: (0548) 830671
Open: 11-2.30; 6-10.30
Lunchtime and evening meals and snacks
Beers: Flowers Original; Flowers IPA
Garden suitable for children

Furnishings:	★★	Garden:	★★	Cleanliness:	★★★
Comfort:	★★★	Views:	★★	Toilets:	★★
Atmosphere:	★★★	OBT:	★	Parking:	★

Two miles south of Ivybridge, midway between the southern edge of Dartmoor and the sea, lies the village of Ermington. I envy the inhabitants their chance to explore the solitude of the moors in the morning, and the unspoilt coastline south of Holbeton or Kingston in the afternoon. These villages are well off the beaten track of tourism, and a stranger needs a fairly detailed map to find his way around. Ermington is an unprepossessing but ancient place, one of the Hundreds of Saxon England, and was no doubt important in those times for its river which rises ten miles to the north on the high moor. The countryside immediately round about is pleasant but unspectacular. At the northern end of the village, in the traditional spot for a pub – next to the church – you will find the First and Last.

The First and Last is an attractive, smallish, stone-built pub with a warm welcome. The present licensees had only been in charge for a few months when I visited, and had already given the pub a lot of attention, with smart new livery inside and out. It is on the B3211 leading from Ivybridge to nowhere in particular, and there is a certain amount of traffic. However the road is hardly an urban motorway, so the noise problem is not severe.

Inside there are three smallish interconnected rooms, brightly and pleasantly furnished, with cushioned chairs. Outside you will find a medium size, level, garden with a number of tables, chairs and parasols. Separated from the garden by a wall is a small car park, from which one must be very careful rejoining the road. Wheelchair access to the front door seems quite good, and with a little perseverence the garden should also be attainable.

Apart from the First and Last, the major attraction of Ermington seems to be its church. Rather like that in Holbeton two or three miles to the south-west, it appears far grander than the scale or demeanour of the village warrants. The parish church of St Peter and St Paul has a Norman inner arch to the main door, with the rest of the building somewhat later. The famous crooked spire, which is strikingly out of true as you approach up the churchyard path, was originally built in the early fourteenth century, struck by lightning in the nineteenth, and rebuilt crooked in response to the demands of parishioners. Did I hear someone say that Devon country people were conservative?

HOW TO GET THERE: Ermington lies on the B3211 from Ivybridge, and also on the B3210 which leaves the A379 about 2 miles west of Modbury. If you aim for the spire of Ermington church, you can hardly fail to find the First and Last.

O.S. sheet 202, ref: 639532

39
NORMANDY ARMS
Blackawton, Devon

Free House

Telephone: (080 421) 316
Open: 10.30-2.30; 5.30-11
Lunchtime and evening meals and snacks
Beers* Blackawton Bitter; Inde Coope Burton Ale
Accommodation

Furnishings:	★★★	Garden:	★	Cleanliness:	★★★
Comfort:	★★★	Views:	★★	Toilets:	★★★★
Atmosphere:	★★★	OBT:	★★	Parking:	★

How does a village pub come to change its name from the Commercial Inn to the Normandy Arms? The first part of the answer is relatively easy: Commercial Inn is nowadays unfashionable, and hardly likely to attract a bustling trade. The second part – the choice of Normandy Arms – is a little more surprising, and has a lot to do with local history. For this area of South Devon was very much concerned with preparations for the allied invasion of France in 1944, which started, of course, with landings on the beaches of Normandy.

The village of Blackawton was immersed in the preparations, being one of the villages evacuated in December 1943 to make way for the US Army. I am told that some practice shells landed in the village and did considerable damage. Whether all this is a solid recommendation for a delightful pub I am not quite sure, but it is important to add that although the Normandy Arms has a number of interesting mementos of those days, its atmosphere is otherwise thoroughly peaceful.

The inside of the pub has been attractively furnished and decorated, using dark wood and plain light walls. There are two medium size interconnected bars, with a shared serving area, and a mixture of chairs and settles, some of them cushioned. Assuming you have a few minutes to spare, there are some interesting mementos on the walls, including copies of letters of exhortation from Monty and Ike to their troops, and a requisition order on the homes of all inhabitants of Blackawton and the neighbouring villages. It is easy to sense the happy contrast between Blackawton's past tribulation and its current peace. On a less weighty note, I must recommend the loos, which are excellent.

Outside, there is parking for about 6 cars and a small garden area on the opposite side of the road from the pub, with a few picnic tables. You will find a reasonable amount of additional parking space nearby. The outlook is villagey, with views to the west, although I have too say that I do not find Blackawton especially attractive; it seems a fairly ordinary country village almost big enough to be called a town. But it has the merit of being away from main roads, and surrounded by unspoilt countryside.

If you can combine a visit here with one to the US Army memorial at Slapton Sands about 5 miles to the south-east, you will see the deeds of Blackawton commemorated in stone.

HOW TO GET THERE: Blackawton is best reached from the B3207 which joins the A381 between Halwell and Dartmouth. The Blackawton turning is about 2 miles from Halwell. As you enter the village you will come to a T-junction. Turn right, and the inn is on your left.

An alternative route is from Strete, a village about a mile to the north of Slapton Sands on the A379. The lanes are narrow but fairly straight.

O.S. sheet 202, ref: 807510

40
MILLBROOK INN
South Pool, Devon

Free House

Telephone: (054 853) 581
Open: 11-3; 6-11 (6.30-11 in Winter)
Substantial snacks, lunchtime and evening
Beers: Real Ales
      Churchward's cider
Wines by the glass
Terrace suitable for children

Furnishings:	★★★	Garden:	★★★	Cleanliness:	★★★★
Comfort:	★★★	Views:	★★	Toilets:	★★★★
Atmosphere:	★★★★	OBT:	★★★★	Parking:	★

South Pool may be a little hard to get to, but you will find it a lot harder to tear yourself away. It lies just a few miles from Kingsbridge, in a lovely remote piece of countryside close to the southernmost tip of Devon at Prawle Point. Well off the beaten track, insulated from the rush by some very narrow lanes, this tiny village has its very own creek on the Kingsbridge estuary. It must be a lovely experience to sail up here on a high tide from Salcombe. I suspect, though, that you must have a knack with tide-tables if you are to avoid spending a lot longer in South Pool than you intended!

Descending into the village by road, you will find the Millbrook Inn down near the creek, on the left hand side of the lane. It is a cosy and delightful place with several small rooms, furnished as much like a home as a pub. The impression is of a lot of thought, and care, and the welcome is warm. As you might expect, the seating is comfortable and the loos are not only quaint, but almost luxurious. Out at the back of the pub a small sliver of a terrace fronts directly onto the village stream. Here you may sit, protected from too much sunshine or rain by a huge striped awning, and enjoy a thoroughly rural scene.

Parking is very limited, so you must take pot luck with other visitors, and locals, on the village street. Unfortunately, wheelchair access is also difficult, because of steps, ridges, and rather narrow doorways. The whole scale of South Pool and the Millbrook Inn is somewhat Lilliputian.

You will probably decide to wander down to the stone bridge at the bottom, inspect the thatched cottages, and enjoy the scenery of the creek. If it is low tide, there is a good stroll of a few hundred yards along the southern shore – but you must come back the same way, because the path is a dead end. As you return, look out for the curious barriers at the front doors of several low-lying cottages near the bridge. You may conclude that they are flood defences, although I gather that the stream must be in spate and backed up by a spring tide and southerly gale before the inhabitants feel really threatened. One elderly local confided in me that the barriers were designed not to keep water out, but children and dogs in. Could it be that such an ingenious idea, nurtured in South Pool, has somehow escaped the notice of the outside world?

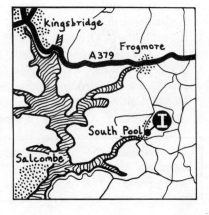

HOW TO GET THERE: Take the sign-posted lane to South Pool from the centre of Frogmore, on the A379 midway between Kingsbridge and Torcross. The lane is narrow and tortuous, with a final steep descent into the village. The pub is easily found towards the end of the main street, on the left. You may find parking easier down near the bridge.

O.S. sheet 202, ref: 777403

41
COACH AND HORSES INN
Buckland Brewer, Devon

Free House

Telephone: (02375) 395
Open: 11-2.30 (Sun 12-3); 5-11 (Sun 7-10.30)
Lunchtime and evening meals and snacks
Limited menu on Mondays and Tuesdays
Beers: Flowers Original; Flowers IPA;
      Draught Guinness; Stella Artois
Wine List; Wines by the glass
Family room; Garden suitable for children
Dogs admitted, but not encouraged
Accommodation (2 double rooms, 1 single)

Furnishings:	★★★	Garden:	★★★	Cleanliness:	★★★
Comfort:	★★★	Views:	★★	Toilets:	★★
Atmosphere:	★★★	OBT:	★★★	Parking:	★★

Church, pub, post office, and perhaps two hundred souls – the recipe for Buckland Brewer is that of a thousand rural villages the length and breadth of England. I cannot claim that this is a particularly attractive or unusual example of the species. But if you have grappled with the traffic of Barnstaple or Bideford, or the summer crush of Clovelly, you may be glad of an hour or two away from it all. In that case I feel sure you will enjoy a visit to the Coach and Horses.

Most villages have at least one fairly easy access route, but Buckland Brewer seems determined to keep itself more or less to itself. Quite a good way is to turn off the A388 about 4 miles south of Bideford. Prepare yourself for a descent into a deeply wooded valley, crossing the unlikely-sounding river Duntz before climbing up again towards the Coach and Horses. By the time you arrive I am confident you will feel well and truly off the beaten track.

The Coach and Horses is an attractive, long, low, thatched pub in the classic Devon style. It has parking for ten or a dozen cars at the back, and there is reasonable extra parking in the village. There's an attractive and generous front terrace, and, at the far end of the building through an arch, a medium-size garden with a wooden climbing frame and a couple of old car tyres suspended on ropes for a children's swing. As you probably gather it is not exactly a gardener's garden, but it serves its purpose well enough.

Through the front door you will find a delightful interior with two smallish bars, and a family room towards the back. There is some danger of knocking head on beam and chest on bar as one enters – such is the intimate scale of the building. I suspect the headroom in much of the bar is about five feet eight, unless you can contrive, without appearing rude or eccentric, to stand head-twixt-beam. Here is the classic old pub atmosphere, and a very local one at that. For my taste there is just about the right amount of everything – furniture, decorations, and seating – the latter mainly fairly comfortable.

If you brush up your German before you arrive, and search for a small brass plate at about head height, you will see that I am not the only "foreigner" who has valued the Coach and Horses and the village of Buckland Brewer.

HOW TO GET THERE: Travelling south on the A388 from Bideford, turn right into a narrow lane at a crossroads about half a mile beyond the village of Monkleigh. The lane descends into a valley after about a mile, goes over a bridge then up again, and reaches Buckland Brewer after about another mile. The inn is on the right, about 300 yards short of the church.

O.S. sheet 190, ref: 422206

42
HALF MOON INN
Sheepwash, Devon

Free House

Telephone: (040 923) 376
Open: 10.30-2.30 (Sun 12-2); 6-11 (Sun 7-10.30)
Lunchtime snacks; Evening meals
Beers★ Courage Best Bitter; Bass Best Bitter;
      Draught Guinness; Tennents Lager
Wine List; House wines in carafe; Wines by the glass
Family room
Dogs admitted
Accommodation (12 double and 2 single rooms)

Furnishings:	★★★★	Garden:	★	Cleanliness:	★★★★
Comfort:	★★★	Views:	★★	Toilets:	★★★
Atmosphere:	★★★★	OBT:	★★★	Parking:	★★

Sheepwash sounded so attractive that I simply had to go and find it. Not surprisingly, it turned out to be very much off the beaten track, half lost in the triangle formed by three country towns of North Devon – Bideford, Hatherleigh, and Holsworthy. For those of us brought up on the idea that England is heavily populated and industrialised, it is a joy to discover such large tracts of countryside. And although the landscape around Sheepwash is unspectacular, and rather flat by Devon standards, there is certainly a great deal of it.

A buzzard circled effortlessly over nearby woodlands as I crossed the river Torridge and entered the village. First impressions, by this route at any rate, are that Sheepwash is a sleepy place, and a little down at heel. But it begins to brighten up towards the village square, perhaps in preparation for the delights to come. For when I saw the Half Moon Inn, and the buildings nearby, I was fairly sure that I had found a gem.

.   The inn is quite large and presumably one of the major enterprises of Sheepwash. Well known to fly fishermen, it is as much a hotel as a pub, and offers substantial accommodation. Parking in the village square is fairly generous, with good level access into the inn for a wheelchair. There is a very small terrace area at the front with a table or two, but, as far as I know, no garden. The entrance to the bar has two rather delightful features: a brass letter box which seems to promise homeliness within; and a painting, divided into scenes of day and night, announcing the pub's opening times on the face of a clock. I was left hoping that liberalisation of the licensing laws would not make such an unusual and attractive feature redundant.

The main bar is admirable. One half of the floor is flagstoned, the other half generously carpeted. There is some very attractive furniture, including wall clocks, a barometer, pictures, and local maps. A big old fireplace is filled – in summer months, anyway – with green plants. Photographs of fishermen with huge salmon suggest that the Torridge is still a highly productive river. The seating is mixed and fairly comfortable, and includes some good bar stools with foot rests. Leading off the main bar is a smaller spillover room, also attractive in a simple way. In short, the whole place has that indefinable sense of what is right in an old inn, with an atmosphere both courteous and relaxed.

HOW TO GET THERE: Turn off the A3072 at Highampton, about 4 miles west of Hatherleigh and 9 miles east of Holsworthy. The turning is in the centre of Highampton, and on an awkward bend if you approach from Hatherleigh. Follow the lane for a mile and a half to Sheepwash, and you will find the Half Moon in the village square.

O.S. sheet 191, ref: 487064

43
CLOVELLY INN

Bratton Clovelly, Devon

Free House

Telephone: (083 787) 348
Open: 11-2.30 (Sun 12-3); 7-11 (Sun 7-10.30)
Lunchtime and evening snacks
Beers: Ushers Best Bitter; Courage Best Bitter;
     Carlsberg Lager
Wines by the glass
Dogs admitted

Furnishings:	★★	Garden:	★	Cleanliness:	★★★
Comfort:	★★★	Views:	★★	Toilets:	★★★
Atmosphere:	★★★	OBT:	★★★★	Parking:	★

If you approach Bratton Clovelly from the crowded A30, you will be enchanted to find how quickly the scene changes into one of rural calm. This is unknown and unexplored West Devon, a long way from the usual tourist tracks. The lane winds for 3 miles up and down and round about, crossing the river Thrushel – a tributary of the Tamar – before climbing into the village. The mighty Thrushel seems to give the inhabitants of Bratton Clovelly some anxious moments, for by the side of the lane is a flood sign which, rather delightfully, can be covered by a hinged flap. I suspect though that the matter is not taken entirely seriously: when I passed by in sunsoaked early September a flood was advertised, yet the river was nowhere to be seen.

The village is quite small and deliciously unspoilt. There is the usual mixture of church, pub, post office-cum-store, and perhaps fifty old houses and cottages. The church has some interesting but slightly overpowering old frescos, a curious little spiral staircase, and a superb Norman font of green Tintagel stone. In its porch you can see some old village stocks, presumably now surplus to requirements, with the cheerful inscription *Fear God, Honour the King*.

You will find the Clovelly Inn past the church at the far end of the village. There are a couple of benches outside on a hard area which also offers limited parking. Fortunately there is quite a bit of additional parking space in the village lanes. Wheelchair access to the pub seems good and level.

Enter, and you will find a medium size bar area divided into two – a smallish "snug" on the left, and a rather larger lounge on the right. The snug's eclectic seating and decoration may pay little attention to current notions of interior design, yet the overall effect contrives to feel both genuine and local. Local, that is, providing you can forgive (you certainly cannot forget!) the enormous head of what I take to be some form of bison adorning the mantelpiece. I can't for the life of me remember his name, but am reasonably sure he comes from elsewhere. If you feel a little overcome by such raw nature, there is a lounge bar on the right also furnished in pleasantly rambling style, with a fine open fireplace and logs piled high.

HOW TO GET THERE: There's a sign saying *Bratton Clovelly 3* on the A30 between Okehampton and Launceston, about 3 miles west of Bridestow. The turning is on a narrow stretch of the main road, and awkward. The lane to Bratton Clovelly is twisty, but straightforward if you follow the signposts. On reaching the village, go past the church and post office. The pub is 200 yards further on.

O.S. sheet 190, ref: 465920

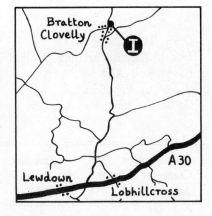

44
BRIDGE INN
Bridgerule, Devon

Free House

Telephone: (028 881) 316
Open: 11.30-2.30; 6-11
Lunchtime and evening meals and snacks
Beers: Real Ales
Wines by the glass
Garden suitable for children

Furnishings:	★★★	Garden:	★★★	Cleanliness:	★★★
Comfort:	★★★	Views:	★★	Toilets:	★
Atmosphere:	★★★	OBT:	★★★	Parking:	★

The normal rule in these parts is that anything east of the Tamar lies in Devon, anything west in Cornwall. But Bridgerule, most of which lies just west of the river, contrives to be in Devon. The county boundary does a curious little westward wiggle just here, and I strongly suspect that the eccentricity reflects an ancient parish or estate boundary which refuses to be bullied by mere geography.

Bridgerule could hardly be described as a beauty spot, but it has a local and unspoilt feel about it. A photograph on the wall of the Bridge Inn – probably taken in about 1890, although I gather that even the locals cannot date it precisely – shows the pub looking like two or three cottages rolled into one, with carts outside in the rough street delivering fresh water. Today the pub looks a lot more inviting, with its newly painted walls and red wagon wheels. Indeed, it has a fair claim to being one of the smartest buildings in the village. There is a small car park for about six cars at the back, and some extra space on the village lanes. Also at the back you will find an attractive raised garden, sloping upwards from the pub and giving quite a lot of extra summer space. Wheelchair access into the pub (but not the garden) appears straightforward.

The inside has been attractively and quite recently redecorated and rearranged. The main bar is of medium size, with a low-beamed ceiling, black woodwork and white paint. The walls have some exposed timbers arranged in an unusual diagonal pattern. There's a good reddish carpet, well-padded green benches against the walls, and some solid wooden chairs with green cushions. A very cosy inner bar, similarly furnished, was formerly a separate room. Decorations include old photographs, some hunting prints, and a glass-fronted cupboard full of silver trophies – formerly the serving bar. The overall feeling of the place is attractive, welcoming, and full of local character. At the far end on the left there is a further room with a pool table. I should add that the gents' loo, external and antediluvian, was being replaced with something much more delectable when I was there, and I imagine it now rates considerably more than a single star!

On the other, truly Devon, side of the Tamar you will find the village church on a hilltop, with a fine tower, diagonally-slated roof, and a lovely sundial.

HOW TO GET THERE: Bridgerule is about 4 miles from Holsworthy, the same from Bude, and lies about 2 miles south of the A3072.

Turn off the A3072 onto the B3254 at Red Post, roughly midway between Holsworthy and Bude, and travel south towards Launceston. After about a mile and a half, turn left to Bridgerule. The road has a couple of sharp turns before reaching the village centre, where you will find the pub on your left.

O.S. sheet 190, ref: 273028

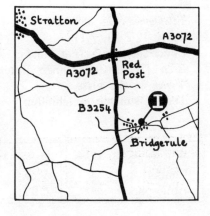

45
BUSH INN

Morwenstow, Cornwall

Free House

Telephone: (028 883) 242
Open: 12-2.30; 7-11
Lunchtime meals (not Sunday, Monday, in Winter); snacks
Beers* St. Austell Tinners Bitter; Hicks Special
Wines by the glass
Terrace suitable for children

Furnishings:	****	Garden:	**	Cleanliness:	***
Comfort:	**	Views:	**	Toilets:	*
Atmosphere:	****	OBT:	***	Parking:	*

My bookshelf holds an illustrated guide to Bude and North C
published by Ward Lock & Co. in 1913 at a price of one shilling. The
words of its section on Morwenstow note that "The Bush Inn is a thatche
cottage, quite unpretentious". It seems that the intervening years have been
relatively kind to little Morwenstow. True, the inn is no longer thatched; but it
is still called The Bush, and it is certainly unpretentious. This, plus the other
delights of a wild and windswept stretch of the North Cornwall coast, are
surely enough to entice you?

Approaching the village along lanes from the busy A39, you will find the inn
on the green at the hamlet of Crosstown, a few hundred yards short of
Morwenstow church. Parking is on and around the green, and a bit
rudimentary. You enter the pub through a yard containing tables and chairs in
fine weather. The main bar is quite small, rather dark, and seething with
character. There are very old wooden settles and tables, a stone fireplace,
wooden casks and handpumps, pewter tankards, and a wooden propeller from
a Gipsy aircraft of the 1930's. An extension bar on a higher level, opened at
busy times, is adorned with miners' lamps and other memorabilia. The
atmosphere is strengthened by the provision of dominoes, cribbage, and darts
– and no piped music. There is also a restaurant. I believe the Bush Inn has
genuine claims to be one of the oldest pubs in Britain, with parts dating back a
thousand years.

Assuming the rough but reasonably flat outside parking area can be
negotiated, then wheelchair access to the yard – and also, I believe, the pub
itself – should present few problems. And while on the subject of the yard, I
should mention that it houses the gents' loo, with the entirely accurate caption
"Behind The Bush". A bit antiquated, but inoffensive.

Even if Morwenstow consisted entirely of the Bush Inn, I should
recommend a visit. But it also has an ancient and fascinating church, and a
vicarage built by the famous Reverend Hawker – "divine, literate, poet, and
eccentric" – who lived and worked here from 1834 to 1875. There is far more to
this story than I can possibly tell. Instead I urge you to seek the place out for
yourself, and walk the few hundred yards from the church to Hawker's Hut on
the wild Cornish clifftops, with their views of Lundy and a restless ocean.

HOW TO GET THERE: Morwenstow
lies about 6 miles north of Bude, and is
signposted from the A39 about 2 miles
north of Kilkhampton. Travelling
through the lanes you first come to the
village of Shop, where you must take a
rather awkward bear-right to Morwenstow. The pub is on the green at Crosstown, about 300 yards short of Morwenstow church.

The Cornwall North Coast Path strikes
inland to pass close to Morwenstow
church, and is an excellent alternative.

O.S. sheet 190, ref: 208151

HOUSE INN

...with, Cornwall

Free House

Telephone: (0840) 770200
Open: Normal pub hours, extended in Summer
Lunchtime and evening meals and snacks
Beers: Flowers IPA; Flowers Original
Family room
Accommodation

Furnishings:	★★★	Garden:	★★★	Cleanliness:	★★
Comfort:	★★★	Views:	★★	Toilets:	★★
Atmosphere:	★★★	OBT:	★★	Parking:	★★

The Mill House Inn is cocooned in a deep tree-lined valley about ½ back from the coast at Trebarwith Strand. It's a cosily protected spot, seems a long way from storm and sea. The pub is a fine old stone building substantial and higgledy-piggledy. At the front is a good hard parking area for about 20 cars – generous at slack times, but much less so in the summer season. Also at the front of the building, facing down the valley, is an attractive terraced front garden on several levels, with wooden tables and white chairs.

The main bars are towards the back, up a flight of steps (which would be hard for a wheelchair). You will find a medium-to-large lounge bar, rather unusually furnished in light pine – chairs, settles, and tables. Most of the seating is cushioned. The walls and available surfaces are covered with a huge variety of memorabilia – silver cups, a geological map, oil and watercolour paintings, a stuffed bird in a cage, framed medals, and caricatures of people who seem to know and appreciate the Mill House Inn (which reminds me: would you dare sit in Jack's Chair?). Twigs and branches adorn the ceiling. I suppose the place lacks a clear decorative theme, but I find the overall effect warm and comfortable enough. Next to the lounge bar is another quite large room with a pool table and a number of small wooden alcoves.

The Mill House Inn is obviously well known. An outside sign advertises it as *AA Inn of the Year 1985*. This is not necessarily a disdavantage – but please don't come expecting Cornish accents and lobster pots. The atmosphere is more of a successful pub in tourist country, and, just as with famous Tintagel nearby, I recommend a visit outside the main holiday season.

Close by, and on the left hand side as you face the sea, an extremely steep lane leads up to Trebarwith hamlet, with its attractive cottages and old-world atmosphere. If you venture up the lane by car, I just hope for your sake that you don't encounter opposition! Much less appealing is the tiny coastal inlet at Trebarwith Strand. Although it's genuine North Cornwall, with superb seas on rough days and fine views out to Gull Rock, it has been spoiled by over-development, and many of the buildings are tatty. Oh! for the attentions of the National Trust.

HOW TO GET THERE: Take the B3263 southwards from Tintagel. Just past the village of Trewarmett turn sharp right to Trebarwith. You will see the inn after about a mile, set back from the road on the right-hand side. There is a very sharp right turn to reach the inn and car park, which are about 100 yards down a narrow lane.

O.S. sheet 200, ref: 058865

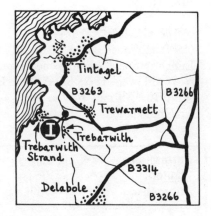

GAVERNE HOTEL

erne, Cornwall

Free House

Telephone: (0208) 880244
Open: Extended hours, but closed January and February
Lunchtime and evening meals and snacks; Cream Teas
Beers: Flowers IPA; St. Austell HSD
Wine List; Wines by the glass
Accommodation

Furnishings:	****	Garden:	*	Cleanliness:	***
Comfort:	***	Views:	***	Toilets:	***
Atmosphere:	****	OBT:	**	Parking:	**

I suppose the fame of its coves and fishing villages has landed Cornwall with more than its fair share of tourism. There are still marvellous stretches of unspoilt coastline, but some of the coastal villages have been rather overpowered by shops, boarding houses, and retirement bungalows. So it is good to find a place which has somehow managed to hold back the tide.

Portgaverne is one rocky headland away from its better known neighbour, Port Isaac. I greatly prefer it – both for its more intimate scale, and for the lack of commercialism. There are perhaps 50 old houses and cottages arranged along a narrow valley leading back from the coast, with the Portgaverne hotel in just the right spot next to the sea. Here are boats pulled up on the foreshore, a fairly small and lovely bay, and not a shop in sight selling imported pottery or T-shirts.

The lounge bar of the hotel is delightful, and open to non-residents. You cross the threshold onto a fine floor of Delabole slate, worn sleek by generations of Portgaverne shoes. The serving area on the left is small, and decorated with old seafaring photographs. I love the ones of Port Isaac lifeboat being manhandled through the narrow streets – as if the crew didn't have more than enough to do at sea! On the right is a comfortable lounge area with a selection of watercolours – all for sale – by local artists. And if you go through the doorway towards the back of the building, you will discover two diminutive rooms, each holding just four or five, which further add to the hotel's charm. There are more nautical photographs, and the inner room, windowless and cavernous, is lit only by the glow from two ship models set in glass cases in the wall.

The hotel has its own car park up a side lane, sufficient for perhaps 20 cars. However I assume it is often filled up by the residents. There is additional parking for a few cars in the lane immediately outside the hotel, and in a small public park just over the road. A wheelchair user might find the two steps to the front door a little daunting.

I didn't discover a garden, unless the tiny fenced lawn next to the hotel is for the use of patrons. It hardly matters anyway. The shore is only 20 yards away, and there is also a miniature public garden with a couple of seats just above it.

Given our increasing awareness of the natural environment, perhaps the main threat to Portgaverne's sanity has passed. I cannot be alone in hoping so.

HOW TO GET THERE: Portgaverne is about half a mile from Port Isaac. If you take the B3267 to Port Isaac, go as far as you can through the village towards the sea, then turn right towards Portgaverne. The hotel is at the head of Portgaverne bay.

Alternatively, approach from the north on the B3314 and take the signposted turning to Portgaverne about 3 miles south of Delabole.

O.S. sheet 200, ref: 004807

48

CORNISH ARMS

St. Merryn, Cornwall

St. Austell

Telephone: (0841) 520288
Open: 11-3 (Sun 12-3); 6-11 (Sun 7-10)
Meals and snacks (May to October, and Public Holidays)
Beers: St. Austell Tinners; Bosuns Bitter; Duchy
Wine List; House wines; Wines by the glass
Dogs admitted at landlord's discretion

Furnishings:	★★★	Garden:	★★	Cleanliness:	★★★
Comfort:	★★	Views:	★★★	Toilets:	★★
Atmosphere:	★★★	OBT:	★	Parking:	★★★★

Many Cornish villages have a "churchtown", and St. Merryn is no exception. In this, the ancient end of the village, you will find the church and vicarage, some cottages, a farm or two, and the Cornish Arms. It is a simple unspoiled place in hilly country, which lies within easy reach of Padstow, the beautiful Camel estuary, and some of the finest cliff scenery and beaches in north Cornwall. Since the pub faces onto the coastal road between Padstow and Newquay, I suppose its off-the-beaten-track status is somewhat compromised. I nevertheless put in a plea that the road is hardly an urban motorway, and that it carries modest traffic except in the height of summer.

The Cornish Arms has an excellent car park at one side for about 50 cars, and a small green area at the back with a few picnic tables overlooking rolling countryside. There are ten more tables on a front terrace facing the church, and access from the car park looks good and level for a wheelchair.

The front door opens into an attractive main bar divided in two. One part has a slate floor and open fire (well and truly alight in late October!), plus a table and a few chairs. To the right is a larger, more comfortable area – reddish carpet, beamed ceiling, cream-painted walls, plus a large stone wall and fireplace at the far end. There are wooden benches all around, padded red. The red-shaded wall lights and dark slatey tones of the local stone give the room a slightly subdued, yet cosy, feeling. A wooden shield on the wall celebrates the pub's links with Royal Naval Air Station (RNAS) St. Merryn, whose first wardroom was based here in 1940.

At the left hand end of the building – a later addition – is a substantial extra bar with pool table and games machines, unusually welcoming and well-carpeted. I suspect that a lot of the pub's business is conducted here.

St. Merryn church is vast and rather beautiful, with wild and windswept views over the countryside to the east. Inside you can see a marvellous Royal Arms of Charles the Second, made in plaster in 1662 by a man of Barnstaple and recently restored to its full glory.

Three quarters of a mile out of St. Merryn on the road towards Padstow, you will find a lane marked to Harlyn Bay. It winds gently down for a mile or so through undulating countryside, to reveal a lovely bay backed by low headlands and, at low tide, a fine stretch of golden sand.

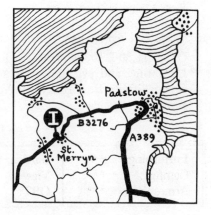

HOW TO GET THERE: St. Merryn is about 2 miles from Padstow, on the B3276 towards Newquay. The Cornish Arms is in the Churchtown end of the village, nearer to Padstow. It is easily found almost opposite the church, on a bend in the road.

O.S. sheet 200, ref: 887743

49
OLD INN
St. Breward, Cornwall

Free House

Telephone: (0208) 850711
Open: 11.30-2.30; 6-10.30
Lunchtime and evening meals and snacks
*Beers** Ushers Best Bitter; Ruddles County
Wines by the glass

Furnishings:	★★★	Garden:	★	Cleanliness:	★★★
Comfort:	★★★	Views:	★★	Toilets:	★★★
Atmosphere:	★★★	OBT:	★★★	Parking:	★★

Unless you realise that St. Breward's church is tacked high up against the slopes of Bodmin Moor and visible from several miles away, the village can take some finding. It is signposted from several places on the B3226 south of Camelford, but you must sooner or later tackle a maze of narrow lanes which seem to have no clear sense of purpose. I can only add: press on, aim for the high ground, and keep a watchful eye on that church tower. The Old Inn is almost in its shadow.

In many ways it is the true Cornwall: no souvenir shops, no candy floss, no groaning car parks. Just a rather craggy, unpretentious, village with long views to the coast in front of it, and the freedom of the moor behind.

The Old Inn is delightfully unfussy. Its inside walls are partly stone, partly white, and topped with low beamed ceilings. The main bar divides more or less in half: at the front, an uncluttered area with a superb Delabole slate floor, its austerity relieved by a snatch of carpet, an open fireplace, and a game of darts; behind, a similar area given over to tables and benches with comfortable cushions, where I was cheerfully served a good snack lunch embarrassingly close to closing time. This is not a place for delicate china, knick-knacks, or smart gossip; the Old Inn knows what it wants, and feels just right in its setting. Still further to the back of the building, you will find a room with a pool table which presumably springs to life in the evenings.

There's quite good parking for a dozen cars, with more space available nearby. Plonked in the middle of the car park, and protected from it by its very own stone wall, is a tiny patch of green with a few picnic tables – and there's another table or two in front of the pub. Wheelchair access from the car park to the pub and garden seems straightforward.

The outlook from the pub does little justice to St. Breward's elevation, but if you stroll a few hundred yards up the road past the church you will find a common with sweeping views towards the sea. Face north-west, and you can make out the village of Delabole against the skyline, underscored by the gash of its vast quarry. It is definitely worth a visit. Not only will you get a feel for an historic local industry, but you can inspect slate tiles, stones, and paving hard-won from Cornish ground, which cost little more than coal yet last a hundred years.

HOW TO GET THERE: St. Breward is signposted at several points on the B3226 south of Camelford. The lanes are narrow. Aim for the high ground and the church tower!

The pub itself is advertised from one of these points. Following this route, you will pass an isolated farm, cross a bridge, then go up a steep hill with a hairpin bend. The pub is at the top on your left.

St. Breward is also signposted from the A30 east of Bodmin.

O.S. sheet 200, ref: 098773

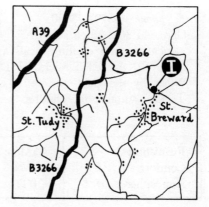

50

CROWS NEST INN

Crows Nest, Cornwall

St. Austell

Telephone: (0579) 45930
Open: 11.30-2.30; 6.30-10.30
Lunchtime and evening meals and snacks
Beers: St. Austell Tinners; HSD
Wines by the glass
Terrace suitable for children

Furnishings:	★★	Garden:	★★	Cleanliness:	★★★
Comfort:	★★	Views:	★★	Toilets:	★★
Atmosphere:	★★★	OBT:	★★★	Parking:	★★★

Inland Cornwall may not always be pretty, but it is nearly always interesting. Ancient burial chambers and stone circles, old mine workings and engine houses – if such stark relics of the county's past appeal to you, I would like to prescribe at least half a day in and around Crow's Nest. But please don't rely on the AA Members' Handbook or the West Country Tourist Board to tell you how to find it!

The Crow's Nest Inn manages a double: delightfully set in a pretty hamlet on the edge of Bodmin Moor; and within a stone's throw of some fascinating relics spanning four thousand years. The inn itself is a fine old building, newly painted white. There's a terrace at the front with about half a dozen picnic tables, a good car park for about 25 cars, and level access for a wheelchair. The road outside is not a busy one, so there is little unwanted noise. Caradon Hill, one of the highest points on Bodmin Moor and studded with old mine workings, rises up immediately behind. Apart from its rather brooding presence, the hamlet seems a gentle place.

Inside you will find a long, slim, bar divided along its centre. The left-hand side boasts a veritable sea of horse brasses hanging from low beams, comfy cushions on dark wooden chairs and window seats, and some evocative old photographs. My favourite shows a childrens' Sunday-school outing at the turn of the century, with the schoolmates in open mine trucks hauled by the steam engine *Caradon*. Close second comes the portrait of the barber at the Phoenix mine attending one of his customers. The other end of the bar, served from the same bar counter, is furnished to a similar standard, but decorated in more nautical style – somehow less satisfactory, given the overwhelming importance of mining to the neighbourhood.

A mile to the north of the pub, on higher and more forbidding ground, stands the old mining village of Minions. Its open moorland is covered with mine workings, derelict engine houses, and much more ancient things – three stone circles known as "The Hurlers", plus the "Cheesewring", and numerous prehistoric tumuli. I can only recommend that you go and explore this fascinating area for yourself. And if you have an appetite for more, there is, just half a mile from Crow's Nest in the opposite direction, a 4,000-year-old burial tomb called Trethevy Quoit, with a huge top stone inclined at an unlikely angle to the horizontal.

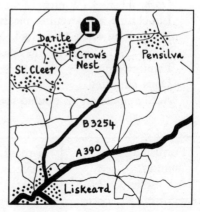

HOW TO GET THERE: Take the B3254 out of Liskeard to the north. After about 4 miles you will come to a large area of common ground on your left, near the top of a hill. The pub is signposted from here, to the left. Go along the lane for about a mile towards Darite, and you will see the pub on your right-hand side.

O.S. sheet 201, ref: 264693

115

51
CARPENTERS ARMS
Metherell, Cornwall

Free House

Telephone: (0579) 50242
Open: 11.30-3 (Winter 12-3); 6.30-11 (Winter 7-11)
Lunchtime and evening meals and snacks
Beers: Wadworth 6X; Hook Norton Ales; Butcombe Bitter
Wine List; Wines by the glass
Family room
Dogs admitted
Accommodation (2 double rooms)

Furnishings:	★★★	Garden:	★★	Cleanliness:	★★★
Comfort:	★★★	Views:	★★	Toilets:	★
Atmosphere:	★★★★	OBT:	★★★	Parking:	★

It must be rare to find an English country pub which is signposted from the Falkland Islands and has figured in *The Times*. I leave you to fill in the details for yourself, by visiting the Carpenters Arms at Metherell. Not that it is the only reason for my recommendation, for the pub is a very delightful one, tucked away in a charming village.

Metherell is in East Cornwall, not far from Callington, and it is inland. There are no glimpses of the sea, or rocky headlands, or wild moors. Instead you will find a sheltered, intimate, place with a wealth of enviable cottages set in scented gardens and narrow lanes. Metherell could do worse than twin itself with Lilliput.

From the outside the Carpenters Arms also looks diminutive - a front terrace which might with luck seat eight or ten, complete with a genuine well, some slightly rickety wooden furniture, and lovely flowers. The outlook is attractively villagey, but enclosed. As you enter the front door, you realise that the pub is surprisingly large, because the basic building (dating from the early 1400's) has been extended to the right to provide a new lounge bar and restaurant. I must say that the whole thing has been carefully and sensitively done.

The old public bar on the left has a superb slate floor, and comes complete with a "snug". The larger lounge bar has some comfortable casual seating, but is mainly arranged in restaurant style. I imagine they can sit 45 people down to a meal here without frayed tempers, to enjoy an extensive menu which includes children's meals and vegetarian dishes. There is a good selection of decorations and ornaments, at just about the right intensity, and the overall effect is very welcoming. It really is very difficult to fault this lovely pub – except perhaps for the outside gents' loo, which is less than luxurious. Incidentally, apart from a steep ramp to the front door, wheelchair access seems reasonable.

Parking is a problem in Metherell. There is space for about 8 cars immediately in front of the pub, but otherwise you will have to do the best you can in the narrow village streets. I know what it is like to be hemmed in by the beer delivery lorry, which was quite unsuited to its task!

The National Trust house at Cotehele is close by, and the views from Kit Hill, two miles to the north-west, are superb.

HOW TO GET THERE: Turn off the A390 a few hundred yards east of the Callington bypass, following a sign saying *Harrowbarrow 2*. After two miles turn left at the T-junction in Harrowbarrow, then almost immediately right. Metherell is a further mile, and you will see a sign for the pub at a small crossroads. Turn right, and the pub is 200 yards down the lane, in its own little side lane (a dead end) on the left.

O.S. sheet 201, ref: 409694

117

52
SPANIARDS INN

Cargreen, Cornwall

Free House

Telephone: (0752) 842830
Open: 11-2.30 (Sun 12-3); 6-11 (Sun 7-10.30)
Snacks; Sunday lunches; Evening meals, Wednesday-Saturday
Beers: Wadworth 6X; Fullers London Pride;
     St. Austell Ales; Spaniards Ale
Wine List; Wines by the glass
Terrace suitable for children
Dogs admitted
Accommodation (3 double rooms, 2 family rooms)

Furnishings:	★★	Garden:	★★	Cleanliness:	★★
Comfort:	★★★	Views:	★★★★	Toilets:	★★★
Atmosphere:	★★★	OBT:	★★	Parking:	★★

The river Tamar – that clean, clear, dividing line between Devon and Cornwall – provides a fine setting for the Spaniards Inn at Cargreen. From the terrace, with your feet firmly planted in Cornwall, you can gaze across the water towards Devon fields, and ignore the problems of Plymouth just four miles to the south. Cargreen is a sleepy little place, which manages to feel just pleasantly behind the times.

The Spaniards Inn looks quaint and compact from the front, but it has been extended at the side and back, and is, in fact, quite an establishment. I suspect its charms are well known in Plymouth and Saltash, and that it attracts a lot of weekend trade in high summer. One advantage of its extension is that the side terrace, which looks out over the Tamar, is quite large. A minor disadvantage – apart from a certain loss of intimacy – is that the pub has about the longest walk from the bar to the gents' loo of any pub I know. However, at least when you arrive the amenities are very fair and reasonable!

Inside, there's a long lounge bar on the right furnished in a mix of styles, with comfortable seating, leading back towards the restaurant. The rather smaller public bar is on the left. As I have already implied, the main attraction to me is the Spaniards' terrace, with fine views of the river. The terrace furniture, rather mixed in style and condition, includes some marvellous granite tables and seats – perhaps not the softest thing you have ever sat on, but surely the most permanent.

Car parking arrangements are fairly good. The main street outside the pub is wide and long, and there's also a pub car park for about 20 cars between the building and the Tamar, on a lower level so the views are not obstructed. Unfortunately there was a certain amount of junk and builder's rubble towards the back of the car park when I was there – perhaps a passing problem. Wheelchair access looks good from the street to the terrace, but there is a six-inch step down at the front door.

If you have children with you and need a diversion, I suggest you stroll 200 yards up the main street, turn left into a narrow lane when you reach the village notice board, pass some lovely cottages, and find the playground so generously provided by the local council. It has swings, slide, seasaw and climbing frames, some lush meadow grass (no dogs!), and surely about the best outlook of any playground in the Kingdom.

HOW TO GET THERE: Cargreen is easily reached from Paynter's Cross on the A388 about 3 miles north of Saltash and 4 miles south of Callington. The lane is well signposted. Follow it for about two and a half miles, then turn left to Cargreen. The inn is at the end of the main village street, beside the Tamar.

O.S. sheet 201, ref: 436626

53
CROWN
Lanlivery, Cornwall

Free House

Telephone: (0208) 872707
Open: 11.30-2.30; 6.30-11
Lunchtime and evening meals and snacks
Beers* Draught Bass; Guest beers
Wine List; Wines by the glass
Garden suitable for children
Accommodation

Furnishings:	★★★★	Garden:	★★★	Cleanliness:	★★★★
Comfort:	★★★★	Views:	★★★	Toilets:	★★★
Atmosphere:	★★★★	OBT:	★★	Parking:	★★★

A mile west of Lostwithiel, and three miles south of the National Trust's house and park on the river Fowey at Lanhydrock, you will find the small village of Lanlivery. I did not discover much more to Lanlivery than a church, a fine Victorian school building, some very attractive rolling farmland – and a superb country inn.

The Crown looks like a very large old farmhouse, excellently maintained, with its back to the road. You enter the front door, so to speak, through the back garden, which is quite large and has a number of picnic tables with parasols. As soon as you get inside you will see that it is a delightful place with black timbers and white walls, softened by red in both seating and carpets. There are several interconnected bar areas: a small, slate-floored, one near the entrance; two medium size lounge bars on the right, one perhaps better described as a restaurant; and another small carpeted bar towards the back. All are spotlessly clean and beautifully furnished. The seating is comfortable, with generous cushions, and there are some particularly soft and enveloping red chairs plus a sofa in one of the lounges. This is a charming and civilised place.

The car park at the side is roughly surfaced but very generous, and must hold about 50 cars. There is a long flight of steps from it down into the garden, which would, I imagine, be impossible for a wheelchair. However if you go towards the back of the car park you will find a narrower path, almost hidden by bushes, which should be a great deal easier.

Like the churches of so many tiny villages, the one in Lanlivery is huge and lovely. Photos displayed inside suggest that the parishioners are having to dig deep into their pockets for repairs. There are fine wooden carvings on the ceilings, and a framed declaration by Charles the First thanking the people of Cornwall for their support against a well-armed opposition. It must be eight feet high and has clearly been there for a very long time.

If you want some exercise there is a public footpath starting opposite the church, and alongside the Crown, to Luxulyan. If the rolling countryside visible from the back of the inn is anything to go by, it must be a pleasant stroll.

Lanlivery is hardly the most exciting place in Cornwall, but you will find it hard to better the Crown if you want a delightful inn in rural surroundings.

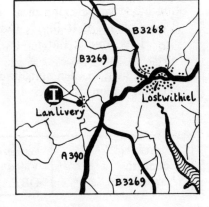

HOW TO GET THERE: Lanlivery is well signposted from the A390 about a mile west of Lostwithiel, and from the B3269 between Lostwithiel and Bodmin. On reaching the village you will find the Crown at its centre, next to the church.

O.S. sheet 200, ref: 080591

54

FISHERMANS ARMS

Golant, Cornwall

Free House

Telephone: (072 683) 2453
Open: 11.30-2.30; 6.30-10.30
Lunchtime and evening meals and snacks
Beers: Courage Best Bitter; Courage Directors;
     John Smiths Bitter
Wines by the glass
Family room; Garden suitable for children
Accommodation

Furnishings:	★★	Garden:	★★★	Cleanliness:	★★★
Comfort:	★★★	Views:	★★★★	Toilets:	★
Atmosphere:	★★★	OBT:	★★★	Parking:	★

Road will not flood again until 7 pm on Thursday 15th - the notice outside the Fishermans Arms, kept up-to-date in chalk, convinced me that my visit would not be watery. It was just as well, for I had parked at the edge of the creek and needed peace to explore the delights of Golant. And I assure you that delights there are, in abundance.

The village is halfway up the Fowey estuary and evokes childhood memories of summers filled with boats and butterflies. I suppose it may not seem that way to the locals; but to the rest of us, compelled to lead more hectic lives, places like Golant are a tonic.

The pub is right beside the creek, itself an offshoot of the river Fowey and separated from it, rather surprisingly, by a railway line. My Ordnance Survey map suggests the line is a "freight line, siding, or tramway", but whatever it does, it doesn't seem to do it very often, and I doubt if it ever gave Golantians sleepless nights. Apart from this single-track concession to speed, the scene is taken up with the delightful trappings of the river Fowey and its waterborne traffic. A short stroll along the lane you will find small boatbuilding workshops, where one-man-bands survive by substituting personal attention for advanced technology. I should warn that Golant has narrow lanes, and the pub's private park is only sufficient for four or five cars. A wheelchair user must negotiate a slope to the front door, and a few low steps or ridges thereafter.

The inside of the Fishermans Arms is fairly small. On the left of the front door there is a family room, furnished in 1950's fashion and reasonably comfy. The main bar on the right is long and narrow, with a mix of chairs and well-cushioned seats. It boasts a mass of decorative items – brass, mugs, old photos, and rigging blocks; a tropical fish tank, an old piano, an even older stove. There's also a notice from Dartmoor prison, dated 1880 or thereabouts, releasing a native of Halifax who had just done seven years for stealing half a hundredweight of iron. I suppose it is all a bit topheavy, yet I find the overall effect homely enough.

For me the main delight is the terrace with its six white tables, and the garden with picnic furniture just below. Try, if you possibly can, to go on a fine day when the tide is up (but not too high!), and enjoy what must be one of the most attractive small waterside pubs in Britain.

HOW TO GET THERE: Golant is well signposted from the B3269 about 4 miles south of Lostwithiel. The lane is narrow, and finally winds down through woods into the village. Go down to the water's edge, turn right, and the pub is almost immediately on your right.

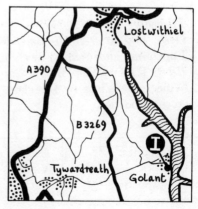

O.S. sheet 200, ref: 123547

55

MINERS ARMS

Mithian, Cornwall

Cornish Brewery

Telephone: (087 255) 2375
Open: 11-2.30; 7-10.30 (Extended hours in Summer)
Lunchtime and evening meals and snacks
Beers: JD Dry Hop Bitter; Cornish Original
Wine List; Wines by the glass
Accommodation

Furnishings:	★★	Garden:	★★	Cleanliness:	★★★
Comfort:	★★★	Views:	★	Toilets:	★★
Atmosphere:	★★★	OBT:	★★	Parking:	★★★

It seems only right that at least one of the Cornish pubs featured here should be called the Miners Arms. This one lies within easy reach of Wheal Coates, Wheal Kitty, Wheal Jane, and the extraordinary tin mining area between Truro and Redruth which is peppered with old mine workings and engine houses. Approaching the Miners Arms at Mithian from the south, you can hardly fail to notice this historic legacy. And if you have a little time to spare, I hope you will explore some of the surviving relics of Cornwall's greatest industry.

Not that mining past or present dominates the immediate surroundings of the Miners Arms. Mithian nowadays seems a gentle country village, with some pretty cottages set in a rural calm. The front of the pub has a small cobblestone terrace with a few picnic tables. A short track at the side leads to a roughish car park for about 15 cars, with a field beyond providing an extremely generous overspill area. At the other side of the pub, approached via a back gate, is a diminutive garden with a couple of rickety picnic tables, enveloped by trees. Wheelchair access into the pub seems good.

The inside is cosy, friendly, a bit higgledy-piggledy, and fairly small. As you might expect of ex-mining country, it is not at all pretentious. There's a small bar, almost a snug, with wooden furniture and a large picture of Queen Elizabeth the First. The lounge bar has a good carpet, very dark woodwork, cream ceilings and walls with some stonework showing, and, for good measure, two or three old mining picks. Green upholstered benches provide comfortable seating all round, and there are four or five tables and some wooden stools. The small restaurant along the corridor looks most attractive and welcoming. I believe there's also a stone-built cellar bar and darts room beneath, which is presumably open at busy times.

If you wish to explore some local mining relics, I have two suggestions. The first is to visit the mighty pumping engines preserved by the National Trust at East Pool, about 7 miles down the A30 between Redruth and Camborne. The second, a rather nearer alternative, is to seek out the cliff edge just west of St. Agnes Beacon which supports the pumping engine house of the Towanroath shaft, built in about 1860 to serve the ancient Wheal Coates mine – surely one of the most dramatic tributes to the indomitable spirit of the Cornish miner.

HOW TO GET THERE: Mithian lies just off the B3285 between St. Agnes and Perranporth, and is signposted about a mile and a half out of St. Agnes. You will find the pub at the village crossroads.

Alternatively, if you are coming from the A30 or from Truro, take the B3277 to St. Agnes. After about 500 yards, turn right into a well-signposted lane to Mithian.

O.S. sheet 204, ref: 745506

56

CROWN INN

St. Ewe, Cornwall

St. Austell

Telephone: (0726) 843322
Open: 11-3; 6-11
Lunchtime and evening meals and snacks
Beers: St. Austell Tinners; St. Austell HSD
Wine List; Wines by the glass
Children allowed in eating areas, and in garden
Accommodation

Furnishings:	★★★★	Garden:	★★★	Cleanliness:	★★★★
Comfort:	★★★	Views:	★★	Toilets:	★★
Atmosphere:	★★★★	OBT:	★★★	Parking:	★★

The village of St. Ewe is a few miles inland from Mevagissey, and very much off Cornwall's beaten tracks. I can thoroughly recommend it as an antidote against traffic or tourists. However I should warn you that, from some directions at least, it is not very well signposted and may prove rather difficult to find.

The Crown Inn is a fine old building, both inside and out. As you approach you will see that it has been made to look about as enticing as it could be, with newly-painted walls and plenty of flowers. You enter directly into a truly delightful lounge bar, with slate floor, beamed ceiling and white walls. Many pubs tend to overdo the decorations, turning themselves more or less into museums; but the Crown has got it just right, with an excellent yet restrained collection of old brass and iron implements, pewter, an old clock, and a fine fireplace. I love the fireplace's wooden mantel, with its removable smoke-control which looks just like a drawer; and the elaborate weight-driven iron spit above. There are wooden tables and uncushioned chairs, plus a few more comfortable benches and window seats. The bar is by no means large, and would probably feel quite full with 15 people. On the right, and directly connected to it, is a restaurant of similar size.

There's a medium-size garden at the back with a few picnic tables, a slightly careworn greenhouse, and a couple of sheds – nice and green and sheltered, although a little less than elegant. The same could reasonably be said of the gents' loo.

If you come by car, you will find two or three parking spaces immediately opposite the pub, and another ten or so further along the road apparently shared with the church. There is quite a bit of extra space in the village itself, within 150 yards of the pub. The village is level, and wheelchair access from the road into the building looks straightforward.

Whether or not you are expert in church architecture, you would probably guess that All Saints church is in south Cornwall because of the palm trees leading to its door. Inside there is a Cornish version of the Lord's Prayer on display, and a note to the effect that one of the 40 recorded rectors was made to resign in 1450 because he couldn't manage Cornish. I imagine you may also wish to read about Jane Carthew – "born at St. Columb, died at St. Ewe" – and her family?

HOW TO GET THERE: From the A390 about 4 miles south-west of St. Austell, take the B3287 towards Tregony. After about 2 miles turn left at a T-junction, leaving the B road (which goes right). Follow signs to Mevagissey for about a mile and a half, then take a steep and narrow right-hand turning signposted to St. Ewe. The inn is near the church and village centre.

O.S. sheet 204, ref: 978462

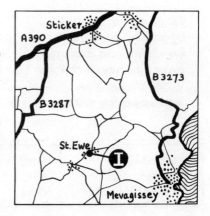

57
TINNERS ARMS
Zennor, Cornwall

Free House

Telephone: (0736) 796927
Open: 12-2.30; 6-10.30
Lunchtime and evening meals and snacks
Beers: St. Austell real ales
Wines by the glass
Terrace-garden suitable for children

Furnishings:	★★	Garden:	★★★	Cleanliness:	★★★
Comfort:	★★	Views:	★★★	Toilets:	★★★
Atmosphere:	★★★	OBT:	★★	Parking:	★

The coastal scenery around Zennor is surely as fine as any in Britain – splendid cliffs and clefts and gullies, backed by gorse and heather-clad slopes. Zennor itself, set three or four hundred yards off the minor road between St. Ives and Land's End, is the sort of north-Cornish village I love to find: very small, a little rough with huge-stoned walls, and largely unspoiled.

The Tinners Arms is, needless to say, next to the church. The adjoining white-walled building, dated 1838, turns out to be not part of the pub itself, but a private house. Immediately behind the pub you will find a farm, and between the two a little footpath leading to the clifftop. There's some parking in the lane nearby, and a village park – emphatically signposted from outside the pub – sixty yards away. Outside, the pub has two terraces; a small one at the front with some white tables and chairs and level access; and a larger south-facing one to the side, approached down two steps and giving lovely views of rolling countryside and sea.

The main bar, quite small, is wooden-boarded with a beamed ceiling, and has a mixture of wooden chairs and tables, and cushioned benches. As befits Zennor, it is unpretentious. On the left there are several additional rooms, former outbuildings, which have recently been done up to provide some very good loos and an additional bar leading onto the side terrace.

Zennor, as I have said, is small. Apart from the pub and church, there are just a few cottages, a cabinet makers' shop housed in an old chapel where you can buy pine furniture and clocks, and the diminutive Wayside Museum founded by one Frederick Christian Hirst (1874-1938). Outside the museum is an old waterwheel, pressed once more into service by a rather unconvincing water supply, and the Zennor Plague Stone – a heavy object with a small depression at its centre, made to hold vinegar during outbreaks of disease. Here money changing hands between Zennor citizens and outsiders was washed. There were apparently major epidemics of cholera in Cornwall in 1832 and 1849.

When you have done with the village itself, do take that path behind the pub towards the cliffs. It's a lovely walk to Zennor Head, finally over a stone stile into National Trust territory amidst majestic scenery.

HOW TO GET THERE: Zennor lies just off the B3306 about 4 miles south-west of St. Ives. Aim for the church, and you cannot fail to see the Tinners Arms.

O.S. sheet 203, ref: 454385

58

LUGGER HOTEL

Portloe, Cornwall

Free House ("restaurant licence" only)

Telephone: (0872) 501322
Open: 12-2.30; 6.30-11.30 (but closed November-March)
Lunchtime snacks; Sunday lunch; Evening meals
Beers: St. Austell Duchy Bitter; Carlsberg Export
Wine List; House wines in carafe; Wines by the glass
Dogs not admitted
Accommodation (16 double rooms, 4 single rooms)

Furnishings:	***	Garden:	**	Cleanliness:	****
Comfort:	****	Views:	****	Toilets:	****
Atmosphere:	****	OBT:	****	Parking:	**

I first went to Portloe over 30 years ago, and remember being enchanted by its diminutive cove with two or three fishing boats winched up the beach, the ceaseless cry of gulls, and the Lugger Hotel's tiny bar overlooking an emerald sea. Then, a few years later, I saw it featured on a British Rail poster advertising get-away-from-it-all holidays, and I recall thinking that that was the end of Portloe. Well either I underestimated the resilience of the locals, or I overestimated the pull of British Rail advertising – because Portloe and the Lugger are still there, essentially unchanged.

You must tackle narrow lanes which finally wind down quite sharply to the sea. As you enter the village you will see a public car park on your right, which you ignore at your peril, because the rest of Portloe is almost impossible for parking. The only exception is the park behind the Lugger itself, which takes about 20 cars, and may offer a safe haven if you arrive at an off-peak time. Otherwise, use the public park, and put a small donation in the honesty box! The walk down to the Lugger is about 200 yards.

The hotel's situation at the waterside is truly delectable. Portloe cove is tiny, and it's hard to see how more than half a dozen boats could ever have come in here. Even so, the village sports a Harbour Commission complete with Harbour Masters – hardly, I suspect, a full-time occupation! Fishing is not what it was, mainly because the lobster stocks have been severely depleted by overfishing; but there are still one or two boats making their owners a living, or half-living, from the sea. The cove is hemmed in by cliffs and headlands, and is just about everything one wants from a Cornish fishing village – everything, that is, except candy floss entertainment. I believe only one new house has been built here since World War Two, and that the remaining buildings are jealously conserved.

You enter the Lugger to find a lounge on the left in which snacks and bar meals are served, and a restaurant straight ahead. The lounge has no less than 20 very comfortable armchairs arranged round several tables, an old fireplace with copper ornaments and "port" and "starboard" lanterns, and a low beamed ceiling. Beyond is a thoroughly enticing smaller bar with doors onto a terrace overlooking the sea. The whole place is excellent, and I simply hope you can choose a fine day and some good company, and revel in its delights.

HOW TO GET THERE: Portloe is on the south Cornish coast about midway between St. Austell and Falmouth. It is signposted (together with Veryan) from the A3078 about 2 miles south of Tregony. A mile or so along the lane, turn left at a T-junction for Portloe. The lane becomes steep and narrow. There's a village car park as you enter. You can try the Lugger's car park – 200 yards further on – at non-peak times.

O.S. sheet 204, ref: 938395

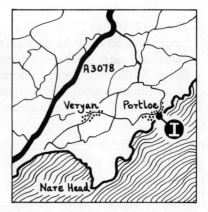

59
PANDORA INN
Restronguet Passage, Cornwall

St. Austell

Telephone: (0326) 72678
Open: 11-2.30; 6-10.30 (Extended hours in Summer)
Lunchtime and evening meals (not Sunday evening); snacks
Beers St. Austell Tinners Bitter; Hicks Special;
      Bosuns Bitter; Draught Bass
Wine List; Wines by the glass

Furnishings:	****	Garden:	***	Cleanliness:	***
Comfort:	***	Views:	****	Toilets:	***
Atmosphere:	****	OBT:	***	Parking:	**

It must be a joy to sail up the Carrick Roads past Falmouth and then, bearing gently to port, to enter narrow-waisted Restronguet creek up at the Pandora Inn. And even for those of us who must settle for less poet transport, this is a delectable spot – a 13th century thatched pub by the waterside, with tables and chairs on a floating pontoon, and a wealth of antique furnishings within.

The last half-mile to Restronguet by road drops steeply and windingly down to the estuary, past delightful houses and cottages. There is very little at the waterside except the Pandora – and certainly no public parking. A rather draconian notice warns that the Pandora's car park, sufficient for about 30 cars, is for the use of patrons only. I can imagine the difficulty of arriving here at busy times and finding it full, but if that particular problem can be avoided the rest is pure delight. At the front of the pub is a terrace with about ten picnic tables, and there are another ten or twelve on the pontoon. I suppose that boating people may need quite a lot of the space at high tide in high summer, but at other times you may sit in perfect peace here, and watch the gentle life of Restronguet float by.

The inside of the Pandora is quite a lot larger than you may suppose, because it has at some time been extended round one side and towards the back. I am sure it is a well-known pub, at least among West Country connoisseurs, and it no doubt has the good trade it so richly deserves. There is a superb series of four or five smallish interconnected bars, with shining stone floors, dark – almost black – beams and woodwork, and white paint between the beams. This rather austere decorative menu is softened by a liberal supply of red-cushioned wall benches, some very good tables and chairs, red-padded stools, and a marvellous collection of old brass and copper, ships' wheels and lanterns, and nautical pictures and prints. I also love the open fireplaces, the superb iron-and-brass range, and the monumental bannister rail leading up the stairs. From a personal point of view, about the only disadvantage is the five-feet-nine to six-feet-three headroom, which puts a premium on sobriety. But even this contributes to the atmosphere.

So long as English pubs, even the well-known ones, manage to maintain such standards of delight, we shall be well served.

HOW TO GET THERE: The inn is about 3 miles north of Falmouth, close to Mylor Bridge. Turn off the A39 towards Mylor about 2 miles north of Penryn. Follow the lane for about a mile, then bear left following signs for Restronguet. After a further mile and a half, turn sharp left (the inn is also signposted at this point). Follow the lane steeply down. The Pandora and its car park are at the bottom.

O.S. sheet 204, ref: 814372

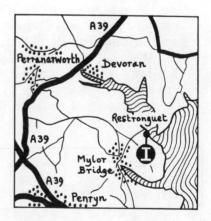

PILCHARDS INN

...ow, Cornwall

Free House

Telephone: (0326) 280256
Open: Normal pub hours in Winter, extended in Summer
Lunchtime snacks only (but not on Fridays in Winter)
Beers: Devenish Dry Hop Bitter; Cornish Original;
   Whitbread Best Bitter; Guest beers in Summer
Wine List; Wines by the glass
Dogs admitted, on lead only
Accommodation (self-contained flat, Easter-October)

Furnishings:	****	Garden:	*	Cleanliness:	***
Comfort:	**	Views:	***	Toilets:	*
Atmosphere:	****	OBT:	****	Parking:	**

Armed with a good map, I decided to approach Porthallow via Mawgan and Manaccan, close to the Helford river. This is lush, almost sub-tropical, country – so very different from the windswept western side of the Lizard. The tiny lanes give occasional glimpses of creeks, and boats, and palm trees. After such sheltered intimacy the village of Porthallow comes as something of a surprise, set in its open valley overlooking the sea.

Porthallow beach is hardly a bucket-and-spade place, not least because of the grey stone, spoil from local quarries, which has for many years been carried round the headlands on storm tides. I gather the locals would like to get rid of it, but if they did I suppose Porthallow would become another village resort with ice cream stalls and the rest. All in all, I prefer it as it is. And if the weather is a little warmer next time, I have promised myself a clear deep-water swim.

The Five Pilchards Inn is almost on the beach, and has been a pub for at least 150 years – initially thatched, but slate-roofed by the 1890's. The main bar, entered via the central doorway, is unusually attractive. Formed from three smaller rooms, it has a lovely warm red-brown atmosphere, with good solid wooden furniture and cushioned benches. It is high-ceilinged for such an old building, with beams and painted boards. Yet it feels quite cosy because (and here is the unusual bit) the surplus headroom has been packed with a superb collection of Porthallow and seafaring mementos. In many pubs such displays appear haphazard, nobody knowing just where the objects come from. But the Five Pilchards' collection is the passion, and delighted interest, of the present landlord – a Porthallow man born and bred; and the personal touch shows.

There's no car park special to the pub itself, but you will find a reasonable amount of space on the lanes nearby, and a village car park with honesty box at the top end of the beach. The approach for a wheelchair seems good and level, apart from two steps at the front door, and I believe the disabled get a special welcome. Outside, there are two or three picnic tables in a small yard.

At the far end of the beach from the pub, a narrow flight of steps leads upwards past a cottage garden to join the coastal path towards Nare Point, with enchanting sea views over to Falmouth and St. Mawes.

HOW TO GET THERE: The easiest route is by the B3293 from Helston to St. Keverne. On reaching St. Keverne, turn hard left along the near side of the village square, into Commercial Road (signposted to Manaccan, Helford, and Porthallow). After half a mile, turn right to Porthallow. The lane is twisty, but quite well signposted. On reaching the village, aim for the beach, and you will find the pub on your right.

O.S. sheet 204, ref: 797232

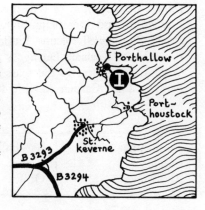

135

61
LOGAN ROCK INN
Treen, Cornwall

St. Austell

Telephone: (0736) 810495
Open: 10.30-2.30; 6-11 (Open all afternoon in Summer)
Lunchtime and evening meals and snacks; Take-away meals
Beers* St. Austell Bosuns Bitter; Tinners;
      Hicks Special; Duchy
Wine List; Wines by the glass
Family room; Garden suitable for children; Will warm baby
food. Dogs allowed, but must be on lead.

Furnishings:	★★★	Garden:	★★	Cleanliness:	★★★
Comfort:	★★	Views:	★★	Toilets:	★★
Atmosphere:	★★★★	OBT:	★★	Parking:	★★

There are a number of logan, or rocking, rocks on the Cornish coast. The one near Treen is famous not only for its size and dramatic location, but also for the temptation it posed to one Lieutenant Goldsmith, RN, in 1824. For this gentleman (if I have understood the tale correctly) pressed nine accomplices into dislodging the stone in an act of late-Georgian vandalism. So great was the public outcry that he was made to replace it – requiring, this time, no less than 50 helpers plus a huge paraphernalia of hoists and lifting tackle. The details of the operation are well described on the walls of the delightful Logan Rock Inn at Treen.

Treen is a curious little stone village spread up a hillside, with perhaps 50 cottages, a Post Office Stores, a public telephone, and a grassy car park (with modest entrance fee) at the far end for those wishing to walk three quarters of a mile to its famous rock. The pub is at the near end of the village, almost as soon as you leave the main road, and close to a lovely little white-boarded tea and gift shop. There's space for a few cars outside the pub on the rather steep lane, plus a fairly rough car park for perhaps another 15. Wheelchair access is reasonably level into the bar – when once you have negotiated the lane – even though the paving leading to the door is slightly uneven.

This is a well known pub, but it is by no means large. On a rather dour evening in early autumn the main bar proved thoroughly welcoming – an open fire with scent of woodsmoke, some good conversation, and a warm glow provided by very attractive lighting. The room has the genuine old pub atmosphere, with a low beamed ceiling, a stone floor partly painted, and some good solid rustic tables and seating including padded benches and window seats. This is, perhaps, no more than one would expect of a pub in the National Trust's care. The overall colour scheme is reddish-brown, with cream walls, some dark wood below, and a certain amount of pine and natural stone. The decorations and pictures are restrained and tasteful – including several old prints describing the Logan Rock's unsettled history.

There's also a small snug bar towards the back of the building, and a family room. Outside, you will find a small walled rear garden with some wooden furniture, and a miniature front terrace with picnic tables.

HOW TO GET THERE: Treen is about 7 miles south-west of Penzance, just off the B3283 leading to Land's End.

About 2 miles beyond St. Buryan on the B3283, in the Land's End direction, there is a very steep hill complete with hairpin bend. Half way up the far side is a sudden, narrow, turning to Treen on your left. The pub is about 150 yards up this lane, preceded by the car park.

O.S. sheet 203, ref: 394231

62
SHIP INN
Porthleven, Cornwall

Courage

Telephone: (03265) 72841
Open: 11.30-2.30 (Sun 12-3); 6.30-11 (Sun 7-10.30)
Lunchtime and evening meals and snacks
Beers: Courage Best Bitter; Courage Directors
Wine List; Wines by the glass
Family room
Dogs admitted

Furnishings:	★★	Garden:	★★	Cleanliness:	★★★
Comfort:	★★	Views:	★★★	Toilets:	★★
Atmosphere:	★★★★	OBT:	★★	Parking:	★

Larger than a village, smaller than a town, Porthleven gives every impression of having a life of its own. Its rugged stone-clad harbour, still very much in use, has rescued countless ships from the south-westerlies which scour this piece of Cornish coastline. And it is still easy to imagine anxious eyes cast seawards from the Ship Inn, seeking mast or light in the gathering storm.

You will find the Ship along an unmade road – perhaps I should say a track – which goes along the western side of the harbour. There is car access of sorts, but it is likely to land you in trouble, especially at busy times, so I recommend you walk instead. Quite apart from saving frayed tempers, my advice will allow you to see and hear and smell something of Porthleven's considerable character. When you reach the Ship, more or less at the harbour mouth, you will find it perched well up on a rocky outcrop, with fine views out to sea. Then, like thousands of seamen and landlubbers before you, you must climb the rough-hewn steps to the bar.

The inside of the pub is fairly small. The main bar, overlooking the sea, has a friendly and quite unpretentious air, with a good mix of locals and visitors – plus a black cat with a blue collar. The walls are a mix of stone and cream, the floor is half-wooden, half slate, and the near-black wooden bar and benches are cheerfully offset by red cushions. On one side there is a fireplace with a huge stone lintel. As you might imagine, there are plenty of seafaring pictures and ornaments, and a menu in which the word Crab appears with some regularity. Rather less expected are several brass plates inscribed with a robust humour. Along a corridor leading to the rear flight of steps is another room desribed as a bar-lounge, which looks more like a small restaurant and serves as a family room. Here too are the loos, complete – in the gents' case at least – with a graffiti board for guests' convenience.

Outside, there's a cavernous cellar bar at road level, open in summer for darts and music. A tiny raised garden with two or three picnic tables overlooks the harbour, and there's an even smaller terrace area below, almost on the road.

The coast beyond the Ship is high and wild, with a fine cliff walk towards Trewavas Head and Praa. On the other side of the harbour starts the huge sweep of Porthleven Sands, lovely for shells and pebbles, but subject to dangerous seas.

HOW TO GET THERE: Porthleven lies about 2 miles south-west of Helston, and is served by the B3304 from the outskirts of Helston, and by a well-signposted turning off the A394 about 3 miles west of Helston.

Park where you can when you reach Porthleven – preferably near the harbour – then go along the western side of the harbour, past a few shops, sheds, and buildings. You will find the Ship after about 250 yards.

O.S. sheet 203, ref: 627256

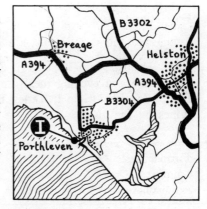

63
HALZEPHRON INN
Gunwalloe, Cornwall

Free House

Telephone: (0326) 240406
Open: 11.30-2.30; 6-10.30 (Fri, Sat, and Summer 6-11)
Lunchtime and evening meals and snacks
Beers Cornish Original; Tetley Bitter
Wines by the glass

Furnishings:	★★★	Garden:	★★	Cleanliness:	★★★
Comfort:	★★	Views:	★★	Toilets:	★★
Atmosphere:	★★★	OBT:	★★★	Parking:	★★

I suppose it is inevitable that an inn called Halzephron, at a place called Gunwalloe in the county of Cornwall, should be associated with smuggling. Normally I steer clear of such tales – like those of ghosts and witches and haunted houses. But in the case of the Halzephron the physical evidence is simply too compelling: an inner wall apparently nine feet shorter than the corresponding outer one, for the very good reason that it hides a vertical shaft, originating in the roof, which proceeds down through the cliff towards the beach. I have it on good authority that the shaft is now disused – not least because it was dynamited by the forces of the law a long time ago.

It is hard to imagine such a chequered history (which included a revoked licence between the wars) as one enters today's trim Halzephron. The first bar is light, low, L-shaped, and of medium size. It has a lot of cream paint, two open fireplaces, a good green-tiled carpet, wooden chairs and padded bench seats, dark tables, and red-shaded wall lights – a bright, pleasing, room in which I assume a smuggler would feel rather less than relaxed. A second bar of similar size, along the narrow building beyond the false wall section, has a somewhat darker, rougher, feel, with its wooden floor and beer-barrel chairs. But even here propriety is assured, for the bar's name is The Revenuers. Halzephron is reformed.

Outside, the pub fronts directly onto the road leading from Gunwalloe village down to Church Cove. There are a few picnic tables on a narrow terrace, and a smallish childrens' play area at the back, beside a car park for about a dozen cars. There is reasonable extra parking in the lane. Wheelchair access looks straightforward.

Almost opposite the pub, two hundred yards down a side-lane (with next to no parking at the end!) is Gunwalloe Cove. It's much less visited than well-known Church Cove, being more exposed to the prevailing south-westerlies. Here you can lose yourself on miles of beach which, at low tide anyway, appear continuous with the great sweep of Porthleven Sands. Half a mile to the south, along the cliff path, is Halzephron Cliff (Hell Cliff), after which the pub is named. And if you have the time, you really should go to Church Cove – much more sheltered, popular with children, and nowadays protected by the National Trust. St. Winwalloe church, half hidden between cliff and dunes, is one of my Cornish favourites.

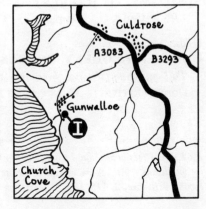

HOW TO GET THERE: Gunwalloe is about 4 miles south of Helston, on the west coast of the Lizard peninsula. Take the A3083 out of Helston, and after about 2 miles turn off to Gunwalloe opposite the far end of Culdrose Airfield. Pass through Gunwalloe village, then follow the road round to the left towards Gunwalloe church and cove. The inn is 300 yards further on, high up and facing the sea.

O.S. sheet 203, ref: 657224

More books from **Ex Libris Press** *are described below:*

Bath/Land's End
WEST COUNTRY TOUR: *Being the Diary of a Tour through the*
  Counties of Somerset, Devon and Cornwall in 1797
  John Skinner   96 pages   £2.95

London/Land's End
GREEN ROAD TO LAND'S END:
  Diary of a Journey on Foot from London to Land's End
  Roger Jones   144 Pages   £2.95

South Devon
TALL SHIPS IN TORBAY:
  A Brief Maritime History of Torquay, Paignton and Brixham
  John Pike   144 pages   £3.95
IRON HORSE TO THE SEA: *Railways in South Devon*
  John Pike   160 pages   £3.95
BETWIXT MOOR AND SEA: *Rambles in South Devon*
  Roger Jones   96 pages   £2.95

Somerset
MENDIP RAMBLES: *12 Walks around the Mendip Hills*
  Peter Wright   96 pages   £2.95
COLLIERS WAY: *History and Walks in the Somerset Coalfield*
  Peter Collier   160 pages   £4.95

Wiltshire
CURIOUS WILTSHIRE
  Mary Delorme   160 pages   £4.95
TOURING GUIDE TO WILTSHIRE VILLAGES
  Margaret Wilson   160 pages   £3.95

Farming Autobiography
SEEDTIME TO HARVEST: *A Farmer's Life*
  Arthur Court   128 pages   £3.95

Ghost Stories
OUR NEIGHBOURLY GHOSTS:
  Tall and Short Stories from the West Country
  Doreen Evelyn   96 pages   £2.95

Ex Libris Press books may be obtained through your local bookshop or direct from
the publisher, post-free on receipt of net price, at 1 The Shambles, Bradford on
Avon, Wiltshire, BA15 1JS. Please ask for a free catalogue.

READERS' COMMENTS

Your comments on any of the inns described in this book are welcome. Please complete the form and post it to me at the address given (no phone calls, please!). I cannot promise to answer all correspondence, but if you want a simple acknowledgement please enclose a stamped addressed envelope.

I should also be very interested to know of other inns and pubs, for possible inclusion in any future editions of the book. They must be in Avon, Somerset, Devon, or Cornwall, lie well away from towns and main roads, and preferably not appear in any of the "Big Name" pub guides.

---

comment form

DELIGHTFUL INNS OFF THE BEATEN TRACK – THE WEST COUNTRY

Please return the completed form to:
Delightful Inns,
c/o Ex Libris Press, Bradford on Avon BA15 1JS.

YOUR NAME:
ADDRESS:

SIGNED: DATE:

COMMENTS

(Please give the name and address of the inn or pub first, in BLOCK CAPITALS, followed by your comments. If you wish to comment on more than one inn, by all means continue overleaf).